HARRY JAMES CARGAS

in conversation with

ELIE WIESEL

PAULIST PRESS
New York, N. Y.   Paramus, N. J.   Toronto, Canada

070020

Library of Congress Catalogue Card Number: 76-11270

Jacket Design: Klaboe/Siwek
Photography: Robert Deutsch

ISBN: 0-8091-0207-2 (Cloth)

Edited for publication by Marianne Papaj

Published by Paulist Press
Editorial Office: 1865 Broadway, New York, New York 10023
Business Office: 400 Sette Drive, Paramus, New Jersey 07652

Printed and Bound in the United States of America

ACKNOWLEDGMENTS
Elie Wiesel, NIGHT. New York, Farrar, Straus & Giroux. Used with
permission
_____, A BEGGAR IN JERUSALEM. New York, Random
House. Used with permission
_____, THE JEWS OF SILENCE. Translated by N. Kozodoy.
New York, Holt, Rinehart & Winston, 1966. Used with permission.
_____, "The Last Return" from LEGENDS OF OUR TIME.
Translated by Stephen Donadio. New York, Holt, Rinehart & Winston, 1968. Used with permission.
_____, THE GATES OF THE FOREST. New York, Holt,
Rinehart & Winston, 1966. Used with permission.
_____, ONE GENERATION AFTER. New York, Random
House, 1970. Used with permission.
Joseph Heller, CATCH 22. New York, Simon & Schuster, 1961. Used
with permission.
Nikos Kazantzakis, THE SAVIORS OF GOD. New York, Simon &
Schuster. Used with permission.
Article by Jim Castelli from NATIONAL CATHOLIC REPORTER,
P. O. Box 218, Kansas City, Mo., 64141. Reprinted with permission.
"What Is A Jew?" from U. S. CATHOLIC/JUBILEE, September,
1971. Used with permission.

The preparation for this book has been one of the holiest experiences of my life. Elie Wiesel, the man, and Elie Wiesel, the writer, has given me this extended sacred moment.

To my father, James Harry Cargas. Only we will know the love and pain that goes with this memorial.

And in dedicatory remembrance of my great—grandmother, Frances Doran, who taught me what love is.

And for my mother, Sophia Cargas Antonov, who comes closer each moment.

Melanie Rosenberg, a former student of mine at Webster College, now living with her family in Israel, was extremely helpful in preparing this manuscript. I thank her for her assistance and her friendship.

Preface

*T*he first time I encountered Elie Wiesel I wept. It was in 1960. An excerpt from *Night* was published in *Jubilee* magazine. The narrator of this memoir told how his father was beaten to death in a Nazi concentration camp while the boy watched. We were living in Manhattan. I taught at St. David's School there and two of my students were the sons of Ed Rice, *Jubilee's* editor. Had I not had this tangential contact with the magazine, I might have overlooked it and not found Wiesel for several more years.

From that instant, Wiesel's work became very special to me. His humanity, his suffering, carried a message from which I did not wish to escape. Somehow this man seemed to embody an important part of my history, a past I had to face, had to examine. The mystery of the Holocaust began to reveal itself. I was being shattered but I was, nevertheless, magnetized to the experience.

I read and re-read all of Wiesel's work that became available to me. He appeared to be writing specifically for me. I felt selfish in demanding more of his work but I seemed to need it to exist. That is, no doubt, why I wrote for Edmonton, Canada's *Western Catholic Reporter* that Wiesel was the world's greatest living author. What I was really saying was that he was the most important living writer for me.

Time passed. I continued to read. Living in Saint Louis in 1971, I moderated a television program called Continuum for the Central Education Network. Wiesel was coming to Saint Louis but I was leaving for a trip to South America on the day he was scheduled to talk. This was clearly going to be a major disappointment. I had heard him once at Washington University and he moved me so much that I could not bring myself to speak to him afterwards; perhaps I felt too comfortable to disturb this messenger from the dead. But two days before my trip the producer of the program called and said Wiesel would be in town the next day, would I care to interview him on the show before I left. I screamed over the phone. The program was set.

We met. We encountered. When the taping was over, I ushered Wiesel out and everyone involved in the production, producer, director, camera personnel, floor director and I all immediately played the remarkable tape back. It was an experience which I'm sure each of us will recall in very moving ways through our lives.

After a number of airings, the program was accidentally erased. However, the text was published in *U.S. Catholic* magazine and forms a part of this book. Some time later I asked Wiesel if he would be interested in collaborating on a book length interview. He accepted the invitation saying that he felt that in Saint Louis we had had "a communion" and we ought to have our conversations and see what would result.

Elie Wiesel does not wish to engage in small talk. His life is short, his vocation immense; so only what is really important should get his attention. (My most painful recollection of him is at a cocktail party arranged by his publisher to launch a new Wiesel novel—at New York's St. Regis. His body was there but his soul seemed to raise the question: Elie, what has this to do with the Holocaust?) So when I walked into his New York apartment, after a year and a half of preparation for these conversations, we barely exchanged greetings. The tape recorder was set up and I immediately asked what may have been an inspired question: "Why are you not mad?"

Where this and some of the other questions I asked came from I cannot be certain. I do know that after the final session, while I was on the elevator going down from Wiesel's apartment, I realized that if I had known the fullness of what the interviews would contain, I would never have done the book. Ordinarily, I would not deliberately ask anyone about a concentration camp experience, about the witnessed murder of a father, or of much else that went into this book.

Now, however, I am satisfied that what was done should have been done. I take no pride in having asked the questions, although I am grateful to have been the individual who represents many of Wiesel's readers in this extended encounter.

Harry James Cargas
Webster College
Saint Louis, 1975

1 / א

*I*n the wagon where the bread had fallen, a real battle had broken out. Men threw themselves on top of each other, stamping on each other, tearing at each other, biting each other. Wild beasts of prey, with animal hatred in their eyes; an extraordinary vitality had seized them, sharpening their teeth and nails.

A crowd of workmen and curious spectators had collected along the train. They had probably never seen a train with such a cargo. Soon, nearly everywhere, pieces of bread were being dropped into the wagons. The audience stared at these skeletons of men, fighting one another to the death for a mouthful.

A piece fell into our wagon. I decided that I would not move. Anyway, I knew that I would never have the strength to *fight with a dozen savage men! Not far away I noticed an old man dragging himself along on all fours. He was trying to disengage himself from the struggle. He held one hand to his heart. I thought at first he had received a blow in the chest. Then I understood; he had a bit of bread under his shirt. With remarkable speed he drew it out and put it to his mouth. His eyes gleamed; a smile, like a grimace, lit up his dead face. And was immediately extinguished. A shadow had just loomed up near him. The shadow threw itself upon him. Felled to the ground, stunned with blows, the old man cried:*

"Meir. Meir, my boy! Don't you recognize me? I'm your father . . . you're hurting me . . . you're killing your father! I've got some bread . . . for you too . . . for you too . . ."

He collapsed. His fist was still clenched around a small piece. He tried to carry it to his mouth. But the other one threw himself upon him and snatched it. The old man again whispered something, let out a rattle, and died amid the general indifference. His son searched him, took the bread, and began to devour it. He was not able to get very far. Two men had seen and hurled themselves upon him. Others joined in. When they withdrew, next to me were two corpses, side by side, the father and the son.

I was fifteen years old.

(*Night* pp. 102-103.)

HJC: Why are you not mad?

 EW: Maybe I am and I don't know it. If I am, I try to know it. When I see the world, the way it is; when I watch the events, the way they unfold; when I think of what is going to happen to our generation, then I have the feeling that I am haunted by that madness—that we all are. Then in order to save myself from *that* madness, I go back to another madness—a holy madness —the one that became a victim, the one that kept us alive for so many centuries, for thousands of years. No, I wouldn't say that I am not mad.

HJC: Silberman talks about your obsession with Life as opposed to

2

Death. He says that your theme is that man owes it to himself not to despair. Does that sum up what you are saying?

EW: Yes and no. I'm obsessed not with Death but with the Dead, with the victims. I constantly ask myself whether I'm not betraying them by speaking or by not speaking enough. At the same time, I am obsessed in a strange way with Life—capital L —with the need for Life for all those who survived. One thing is sure: man today must be obsessed; if he is, there is still hope. If he is passionate, meaning *com*passionate—compassionate with those who want to live, with those who are alive no longer, compassionate with children who are inheriting too many memories, too many fears and guilt feelings—there is hope.

HJC: You mentioned in *Legends* that Moshe the Madman appears in all of your books. Is this a realization of the same kind of thing?

EW: In *The Oath* he is the main character; I bring him back. *Night* was the foundation; all the rest is commentary. In each book, I take one character out of *Night* and give him a refuge, a book, a tale, a name, a destiny of his own. Now has come the time for Moshe but I change many elements: the period, the atmosphere, the events. It's no longer connected directly with the Holocaust. Moshe comes back all the time as a warning, a reminder, an echo and often as an inspiration.

HJC: Would it be fair to say that you oppose individual insanity rather than madness?

EW: Let us say I oppose insanity but I am for madness, individual but not collective madness. When I speak of madness I mean a mystical madness. I am against insanity, generally speaking. I think man should not be insane—man should fight insanity. But from time to time, when there are choices and options to be made and taken, then madness—mystical madness—is important. One has to be mad today, in this time and age, to say certain things and believe that they could make a difference. One has to be mad today to have children and unless you are determined and ready to communicate that madness to your children, then you *are* insane.

HJC: And you are saying this six months after the birth of your first child?

EW: Yes, I say that thinking of him. It is a strange event in my life to have a son, despite or rather *because* of everything. With all my pessimism with regard to the human race, with regard to the future, we have to prolong life.

HJC: I know about your feelings of pessimism, yet, if I might say it, they are tinged with optimism. I want to ask about this. So many writers in the modern era—visionaries, seers—have committed suicide: Mishima, Kawabata, de Montherlant, Hemingway, Pavese, Sylvia Plath, Jarrell, Berryman. Can we deduce anything from this?

EW: I think the reasons and the motivations are not always the same. Some writers commit suicide because they have written their best work and they know they won't write anything else. Others commit suicide because they are attracted to and fascinated by death, which is the case with Mishima. I think Montherlant's suicide is different. He wanted to prove something, to prove his own validity, to prove that he was right: he spoke so much about suicide that he wanted to end his theories and say, "Here I am, the one who confirms them."

There are other literary suicides which one day should be explored by one of our students, yours or mine—writers who wrote about and came from the Holocaust. In the nineteenth century *readers* committed suicide. In the twentieth century it's the *writer*. Take Tadeusz Borowski, a Polish writer, who took his life by gas. Recently a poet in Paris, Paul Celan, committed suicide as did Josef Wulf in Berlin. There was something in the Holocaust which moved the sensitive person to despair. The more sensitive the person, the more desperate he became because he knew that we had reached an end, an end in history, that something happened one generation ago; something that will doom us forever.

At the same time these writers and philosophers and poets felt that they performed a certain task, otherwise they wouldn't be alive; they wouldn't write—their task being that of a witness or a messenger. At one point or another they felt that they had failed. I feel that often: we failed. We did not write to entertain; we didn't write to make money. We didn't write for any accepted purpose except for the extraordinary purpose of saving mankind.

Each writer, each survivor, became the Messiah or at least

the messenger who knew the Messiah and who knew how to bring him. Each one really hoped to save mankind, not only the Jewish people. Here we see that mankind is racing to its death, to its own destruction. What do we conclude? We say that we have not fulfilled our role; we didn't testify in the right way. We didn't do enough; we didn't do it the way it should have been done. So, many writers committed suicide. How many died without even having written the first word? They simply gave up even before writing it.

Recently I reread chronicles written by historians in the ghettos: Ringelblum, Kaplan. They were all young and all became witnesses. They all felt that they had to record events for future generations, the main obsession during the war, so the tales should not be lost or wasted—the experiences should not go astray. I was amazed and astounded by the style. Such an incisive, short style; sometimes sentences of one word. When I read them I understood my own style, why I wrote in such a condensed way.

Actually, I saw myself following in their footsteps. When they began a sentence they could never tell whether they would be alive to finish it: it had to contain everything. We have the same feeling, we who write about that experience. But after you have written the sentence and it leaves you, you wonder, did you say the right thing? Is the substance transmitted? Frequently you have remorse. Something else should have been said instead. Other words should have been used, or none at all.

HJC: But this remorse does not lead you to a state whereby you produce nothing. After you write there is a time before it is published that you could say, "Well, I won't." And yet you do publish. You have this feeling of responsibility—this is what I'm asking.

EW: Absolutely! I accept the remorse. I assume it existentially. I don't have the right not to communicate. If I could communicate what I have to say through not publishing, I would do it. If I could, to use a poetic image, communicate a Silence through silence I would do so. But I cannot. Perhaps I am not strong enough or wise enough. I try to communicate that Silence with words. Nevertheless, I know there is a feeling of failure and a feeling of remorse. I accept all of these feelings but these are my concern and not the reader's. As far as the reader is concerned, I try to give him as much as possible a total picture of what was my past which, ultimately, was his past as well.

HJC: You mention in *One Generation After* that words confuse and you want to escape that confusion. Marshall McLuhan, in one of his earlier books, said that speech acts to separate man from man and mankind from the cosmic unconscious. I think there's a kind of similarity of approach there.

EW: He, I think, mentions it from a linguistic point of view. My approach is a more philosophical one although linguistics is philosophy today. I believe that speech can bring people together while he believes that speech automatically and irrevocably divides people. I think not.

Words can bring man closer to himself, to God, and to others provided the words are the right words. The question is, are they ever the right words? It is not up to us to decide. There are certain responsibilities which are ours. To justify them we need the other person. Only a person whom I try to help can tell me in what way I can help him. I owe him the courtesy to let him decide. He needs the words, not I. If someone tells me that he suffers, I owe him the courtesy to believe him. The motives may be whatever they are but I must believe him. If he says, "I need your words and not your silence," I must give him words. It's up to him to decide whether they are right or not right.

HJC: You're talking about the creative aspect of reading and the relationship that the reader enters into with the author.

EW: Between author and reader there must be a dialogue. When man speaks to God there is a dialogue. The creative process is a strange one: it comes from solitude, it goes to solitude and yet it's a meeting between two solitudes. It is just like man's solitude faced with God's solitude. Once you have this confrontation, you have art and religion and more. You have a certain communion in the best and purest sense of the word. Exactly the same thing happens when you write and someone reads you; your solitude is faced with the reader's and you join with that solitude. When both are sincere, God is there. Whenever one man speaks to another, ultimately he involves God.

6

HJC: A glib example: somebody asked Hemingway what he meant by his latest novel and he responded: "How do I know? I only wrote it." There's at least some of that in your answer, isn't there?

EW: Yes, because there's the unknown. But I *do* know. I know at least part of the answer to what I wanted to say.

HJC: But the reader helps complete, at least for *him*, the meaning of the work.

EW: He brings his own associations to it. It's *his* life. I give him the code. Sometimes I give him a key. But the code applies to *his* text, to *his* life, to *his* destiny. I give him the example, the model, but he brings his own past, his own fears and anguish, his own ambitions.

HJC: There are different kinds of silences—creative and destructive silences—aren't there?

EW: Yes, just as there are different kinds of madnesses. Let's take the problem of suffering because it's one of the elements that moves me to write. If someone suffers and he keeps silent, it can be a good silence. If someone suffers and *I* keep silent, then it's a destructive silence. If we envisage literature and human destiny as endeavors by man to redeem himself, then we must admit the obsession, the overall dominating theme of responsibility, that we are responsible for one another. I am responsible for his or her suffering, for his or her destiny. If not, we are condemned by our solitude forever and it has no meaning. This solitude is a negative, destructive solitude, a self-destructive solitude.

HJC: Clearly a major non-force, if you will, in the world today.

EW: Unfortunately. I feel the world has never been more in danger of self-destruction than now. Never before has man had so many means, possibilities, insane desires and urges to do away with his own destiny. Maybe because he feels guilty for Auschwitz and whatever followed, like Hiroshima. Hiroshima was an attempt of self-destruction. So, we come back to our pessimism.

HJC: You said somewhere that Hiroshima was not possible without Auschwitz.

EW: I don't compare the two. Auschwitz was a unique phenomenon, a unique event, like the revelation at Sinai. But Hiroshima would not have been possible if it hadn't been for Auschwitz. Auschwitz paved the way for all the Hiroshimas in the future.

HJC: Some of the things you said about creative and destructive silences, if I can force those terms into this discussion, apply to the Jews who were destroyed in the Holocaust on the one hand —their silence—and on the other, the silence of the world that witnessed their destruction.

EW: Exactly that. I meant that and the images that you chose are good: the silence of the victims and the silence of the accomplices or the executioners. You have a confrontation of two silences. The silence of the victims was in a weird, unreal, way a constructive silence; it added something to our history. The silence of the accomplices was a destructive one because it destroyed our future.

HJC: When you say, "added something to *our* history," who is the "*our?*"

EW: I mean *our*, yours and mine. When I say "I," I speak as a Jew because I am Jewish and I assume the entire destiny of my people from beginning to now. As a Jew I believe that to be a Jew is to be an opening. But when the Jew is Jewish he speaks on behalf of everybody. Just as you, when you speak as a human being, or as a Christian, when you assume your identity and your past, with all that goes with it, you may speak in everybody's name too.

HJC: In *A Beggar In Jerusalem* a character said he can't assume his manhood without assuming his Jewishness. This is what you're reiterating now.

EW: At one point or another, every person becomes Jewish—the moment he becomes authentic he genuinely—though metaphorically—becomes Jewish. And every Jew is universal the moment he is genuine.

Thomas Merton wrote that it won't be a madman who will push the final button which may destroy us all— rather it is the *sane ones* who, he says, are the more dan-

gerous. First, of course, it is the "sane ones" who prepared the weapons; second, it is the "sane ones" who will
have *"perfectly good reasons*, logical, well adjusted reasons, for firing the shot." (We will remember the com-
manding officer in Vietnam who had to destroy a friendly
village to save it from the Communists.)

The cloistered monk, Thomas Merton, was a man, like
Elie Wiesel, concerned both with holy silence and the insanity of the world. It is not, after all, the mad, the fools
for God, who will really murder for God's sake. Who was
mad in Hitler's Germany? Franz Jagersdatter or Dietrich
Bonhoeffer, on the one hand, who refused to participate
in the Third Reich's very logical and sane approach to
racial purity or, on the other hand, the propagandists who
preached (and the followers who believed) that Adolf
Hitler was the third person of the Christian Trinity? (See
Peter Viereck's *Metapolitics.*)

Joseph Heller gives his answer in that remarkable production, *Catch-22*. ". . . The war was still going on. Men
went mad and were rewarded with medals." The fully
human soldiers in that novel are those trying to escape
the war—Orr and, of course, particularly Yossarian. The
latter is concerned that the enemy is trying to kill him.
His friend, Clevinger, attempts to comfort him:

> "No one's trying to kill you," Clevinger cried.
> "Then why are they shooting at me?" Yossarian
> asked.
> "They're shooting at *everyone*," Clevinger
> answered. "They're trying to kill everyone."
> "And what difference does that make?"

It is clear with whom our sympathies are meant to be
shared in the above dialogue because it is clear which one
is the man of insight. Early in the book, Yossarian thinks
about one aspect of bombing, "That wasn't funny, there
were lots of things that weren't even funnier."

Wiesel, Merton, the fictional Yossarian indeed think alike about what insanity is. It seems to be mob centered. It's as if each were saying, with Ibsen, that the minority is right. The minority alone thinks about things deeply. The minority is not stampeded into a decision whether the subject is an election or a lynching. Only a few persons are willing to risk the trip inward, searching their souls for the meaning of life and their individual relationships to that meaning. The answer to the meaning of life is left to others and Harvey Cox is proven correct: not to decide is to decide. If Wiesel's mad characters in his novels do anything, they *do* decide. Hence, he begins his novel, *The Town Beyond The Wall* with a quotation from Dostoyevski: "I have a plan—to go mad." This purpose indicates choice and is active. Wiesel's people are not *driven* mad. Perhaps some of the other characters are driven sane but Wiesel's madmen are mystically mad people who have decided in favor of God and man. Moshe the beadle, who appears in a number of Wiesel's books, is the absolute of this. Other such characters are Gavriel, in *The Gates Of The Forest*, who gives away his name and adopts the stance of an idiot until he sanctifies Judas in the local passion play and Michael, in *The Town Beyond The Wall*, who willingly duped a kind of madness to save his friend and thus be a witness to man and God.

Wiesel is not unique in attributing to madness a power of perception keener than that of others. Cervantes, Nietzsche, Shakespeare and even certain Scriptural situations come to mind. Don Quixote has broken from the neutral cliches with which most of us are afflicted—he has escaped the muddled, well travelled thought ruts which have entrapped the carriage wheels of most of our minds. And for that he is a hero. As Lionel Trilling has noted, "The impulse to transcend the rational mind would seem to be very deeply rooted in man's nature." Can the reason be that the rational mind is that which has filled us with the illusions of life as O'Neill has rendered it in *The Iceman Cometh*? Octavio Paz is disturbed that we cannot know true history now because "official" history confuses the real and the illusory. Wiesel would insist that this is certain on individual, as well as international, levels.

It is our habit, perhaps, to force onto our existences meanings which they do not have. One who has experienced the Holocaust, however, arrives at the idea of the absurdity, of the meaninglessness of that event. We may, perhaps, only partly agree with Wiesel that the Holocaust has no meaning. I project that for the Jew who experienced the event (even vicariously—and this might include people who are not of the Jewish faith) the Holocaust is clearly meaningless. Events for the person being persecuted frequently can have no meaning. But for the persecutor it is another matter. For Christians, in Christian nations (and others, again vicariously), who, after an apparent tradition of two thousand years of the love of Christ for man, to be able to think of, then construct, and finally even use ovens for human beings—for these people the Holocaust must indeed have a message. In my judgment that message, too, is in Elie Wiesel's novels. Silently, but there.

2 / ב

*S*omewhere a storyteller is bent over a photograph taken by a German, an officer fond of collecting souvenirs. It shows a father and his son, in the middle of a human herd, moving toward the ditch where, a moment later, they will be shot. The father, his left hand on the boy's shoulder, speaks gently while his right hand points to the sky. He is explaining the battle between love and hatred: "You see, my child, we are right now losing that battle." And since the boy does not answer, his father continues: "Know, my son, if gratuitous suffering exists, it is ordained by divine will. Whoever kills, kills God. Each murder is a suicide, with the Eternal eternally the victim."

(*A Beggar in Jerusalem*, p. 208.)

HJC: What does it mean to be a chosen people

EW: Chosen people is actually the people of choices—a choosing people. Mysteries of God are mysteries to me. Why did he choose a people who, at the same time, chose to give him to the entire universe? Maybe because they were the feeblest; maybe because they were the poorest. I don't know why. I know that the choice is still ours. Every Jew must choose himself again and again as a Jew and must choose his God every day and every hour.

Does it mean obligations? Naturally. Does it mean limitations? No. Does it mean seclusion? No. Does it mean isolation? No. It means to deepen our own condition, to put an accent on certain things, a stress on certain values. I would never accept a view that would oppose Jewishness to universalism. An attempt that says that once a Jew is Jewish, he belongs to his people alone and not to others. It's impossible, it's unfeasible and it's not in line with our concept of history.

The example I quoted is a pertinent one. When God said to the Jewish people, "I shall be your God," something unusual happened. He who was the God of the universe chose to be the particular God of the smallest people on earth. But the moment he said it they said, "No. You are our God and also the God of the universe." Which is the only way for a Jew to be Jewish: first he must accept what he is.

In accepting his own condition, his own identity, he gives himself to his people and through it to the entire world, to mankind. Sometimes mankind doesn't accept the Jew of the Jewish image or offering, the Jewish heritage, because mankind prefers a distorted view, a distorted image of the Jew. But then it's a different problem.

HJC: In one novel you say that Jews are God's memory.

EW: As opposed to man's memory.

HJC: What is the meaning of Israel today in the light of what we've just said?

EW: Do you mean Israel the people or Israel the nation?

HJC: The nation.

EW: It's too early to say. If Israel was only twenty-five years old then the whole episode would be nothing but an episode. Israel the nation exists over two thousand *and* twenty-five years or three thousand *and* twenty-five years, so we may draw certain conclusions. I think that the secularists were wrong when they wanted to have a nation like all the others. They were wrong because Israel *cannot* be a nation like all others. It is impossible. It's a counter-sense, it's a non-sense, really, a contradiction in terms.

If, in 1948, the whole idea was to have another nation then it was not necessary to deplace so many refugees and to cause such a turmoil. It wasn't a historic necessity. If it was a way to re-enter history and to correct history then it's something else. The secularists who simply wanted to have a nation—a normal nation—with a normal army and police and diplomacy—no. It needs a mystical connotation. Otherwise, maybe it would fare better but not in the same direction.

Today Israel to me is still an example of what can be done, an example of difference, of variety, of humanity. Israel should be, today, the nation that shows to stronger powers that military victories alone are not real victories, that they ought not to exclude honor and dignity. Victory does not necessarily mean the enemy's defeat and humiliation.

I believe Israel can and should personify a powerful message to the world, a message against the great powers, against China, Russia and America where the process of dehumanization is frightening. Here, through comfort, technology, social progress; in Russia by Communist fear and terror; in China, one doesn't know yet. Here is this small nation that must show that although it is surrounded by enemies, always faced with adversity, it is worthy of the challenge and it can remain human.

HJC: Is it meeting this end?

EW: I don't know. If I compare Israel to what's happening to other nations, then yes. Then I am proud of Israel. Naturally, there are things that I would like Israel to do. I would like Israel to be more aware of suffering that we—here I say "we" although I am not an Israeli, but I identify with Israel—that we have caused. I know it hurts the Israelis. Maybe I don't have the right to say it because they are there and I am here in America but I cannot *not* think of the Arab refugees. I know that Arab leaders are responsible for there being refugees—if it hadn't been for Nasser, or for other Arabs, the problem would not have been as acute; it would have been solved already. I know that they should have done what we have done with our refugees—I know all this. The fact is that there are children born in the refugee camps, and they suffer, and although I am not *directly* responsible—except as a Jew who is identified with Israel—I feel that because they suffer and I don't, there is something wrong. I would like Israel to think about it more and to show more compassion.

But then I understand Israel; it has other worries. Israel has its own survival in mind, naturally, but maybe *we* should do it then. Maybe it should become our task. I have played with an idea for a couple of years but unfortunately I am not an organizer so I cannot do it: to establish an international committee of survivors—Jewish and non-Jewish—who went through the concentration camps—but not Israelis. We should simply come to the Arab refugees and try to help them. We should say, "Listen, we too, we were uprooted. We too, we suffered injustices. We lost more than you did. So let us teach you how one builds on ruins. Let us teach you how one can go on living without rancor and without resentment." I played with the idea for a couple of years but I'm not a politician, never have been and have no ambition to become a public figure. So the idea is an idea. I wish someone would work on it.

HJC: The Jews cannot survive without Israel is something that I heard you say some time ago.

EW: Yes. The Jews could not survive without Israel. But the Jews could not survive today without any other Jewish community. If in 1948 there would have been no Israel, we could have gone on living for centuries and centuries. Since Israel is here and it came—I hate to admit it as the result of the Holocaust if not as a response to it—the disappearance of Israel would mean another Holocaust and our generation is too weak. We could not take another Holocaust. I am persuaded that the disappearance of any large community—let's say in America, Israel, or Russia —would mean the end of the entire people because we are too hurt. Our wounds are open and the trauma is still here. It becomes deeper and deeper with time.

I believe history hasn't exploded all the time-bombs yet.

Just as we have earthquakes, there will be timequakes and the Holocaust will come back, again and again. Should it happen, it will mean the end—mass suicide. But it cannot happen. I don't think it can because for the first time in our history, mankind and the Jewish people follow an identical path. For the first time we share the same history. For two thousand years we were outside; our history was not mankind's history. Here and there, there were common points, common links— great thinkers, writers, physicians. Generally, we ignored the outside world; the outside world either ignored us or tried to kill us. For the first time—maybe it's because of technology, of communication, and because of Israel as a nation that can develop its own weapons and its own means of survival—we have the same history.

HJC: The concept of the Messiah for the contemporary Jew . . . in *The Gates Of The Forest* one of the characters said the Messiah is everywhere. The notion of the Messiah for the modern Jew is a very real one, is it not?

EW: Not only for the modern Jew. The Messiah embodies waiting and hope. The difference between the Jew and the Christian today is that we are still waiting for the Messiah to come. At the same time, we don't know what the Messiah is or who he is. We are told in the Talmud that one of the things created before Creation was the name of the Messiah, a beautiful, mystical, way of saying to us that it's always removed. *We* can bring the Messiah, not God. Only man can bring the Messiah. Only man can bring redemption *to* God. But the name of the Messiah, the beginning of the process, is rooted *in* God. So we search everywhere.

There is a beautiful legend in the Talmud that disciples of various rabbis were discussing what will be the name of the Messiah. And one said Yinon, one said Haninah—all kinds of names were offered, each one claiming that "my teacher" has the name of the Messiah. Were they really quarreling about names, or paying respect to their teachers? They wanted to show that the Messiah will be in all these names. The Messiah will be part of everybody. One thing is clear to me as a Jew— he hasn't come yet.

HJC: Your characters say several times, I think, that each beggar might be the Messiah.

EW: That I take from the Talmud too. Talmud says that the Messiah can be found among the beggars and the sick, at the gates of Rome, which is a striking image. Don't look for the Messiah among the rich; don't look for the Messiah in golden palaces—only among the beggars. I, of course, use my literary license to make it even more precise—every beggar can be the Messiah. Therefore, treat every beggar with respect. Every beggar gives you more than he receives. Ever beggar can become a messenger to you and make you into another messenger.

HJC: Is the Jew more lonely than others?

EW: Yes and no, depending on the periods. Sometimes you feel terribly alone. In times of crisis, despair, danger, we feel terribly, painfully alone. Imagine the Holocaust—there was such a solitude in Europe that even *we* will never know its magnitude. In 1967, when Israel was threatened, the key word that entered my mind again and again was "solitude." Once again, we are alone. When this happens we close our eyes and we see ourselves. Then *among* ourselves we feel better.

The outside world manages to push us back into our own ghetto, so to speak, which is bad. At the same time, it makes the Jew more Jewish, which is good. Actually, it's an ambiguous approach and an ambiguous state of affairs. Ambiguity is the name of our sickness, of everybody's sickness. What are we looking for in life, in existence, in history, in our own being? For the One to do away with ambiguity. The moment the Messiah comes, we are told, everything will be One. We shall all be One. We shall all go back to our source, to our root, or as we say in mysticism, the primary order will be restored and God himself will be united with his presence, with his people. The oneness is the aim and One is the secret.

HJC: Will this coming, could it be the *result* of people coming closer together or will it be the *cause* of the unity? Could it in one sense be the result also?

EW: It can be the result.

HJC: I'm asking—the world has to be worthy of the Messiah.

EW: We have an image which was long misunderstood. The image in the Talmud says that the Messiah will come in either of two cases: the world will be totally just or totally sinful. I resent the second possibility because I wouldn't want to have a Messiah come to a totally corrupt world; the Messiah himself would be unjust and incomplete—a wrong Messiah. But this sentence was misunderstood. What the Talmud meant to say is there will be a time when we will live in extremes with nothing in between. No neutrality. A man will have to choose either to be with the just or with the unjust and not to stand in between, idly waiting. When that will happen, when there will be such an awareness among men that they will have the courage to choose, then the Messiah will come. That means man will be worthy of him. This is the Jewish belief. Here and there a few Hasidic masters, who were sometimes taken in by pessimism, voiced different views. One of them said the Messiah will come when nobody will be waiting for him. He meant it as a desperate outcry: "Look where we are; we are not even waiting for him anymore."

HJC: Does past suffering contribute to being made worthy?

EW: I don't believe in suffering. If suffering was to make man worthy, then the Messiah would have come in 1942, 1943, 1944. For then, surely, we were all worthy. Surely then mankind was divided into just and unjust with no neutrality because the neutral ones were guilty as accomplices. Especially in the free countries like America and Sweden and Switzerland or the Vatican. Surely they were guilty by not helping, by not taking sides or by waiting, by temporizing. On the other hand, the victims were suffering. They knew paroxystic suffering then. If that was the measure, the Messiah would have come.

But suffering does not lead to saintliness. I think suffering is evil. Man is not created in order to suffer. If this were so, then God could not be holy. God does not want man to suffer; man suffers against God. We believe that suffering is not the answer; suffering is only the question. What do we do with it? That is the problem. Our people, since the very beginning, have tried to teach the world not how *not* to suffer because we have suffered all the time, especially during the last two thousand years, but what to do *with* suffering. Not to let it become our master. Not to give in to resignation. Not to let it transform us into generators of sufferings; not to make us increase its own limits, its own dimension. The answer to suffering is surely not more suffering; the answer should be a diminution of suffering. And to say to ourselves that despite the suffering, we can go on, go on believing, hoping, creating.

HJC: The subject of the mystery of suffering is a question that has been with me for as long as I could think about things like that. But you've said it's a mystery. What's the point? In a sense, what is God doing? It isn't just the Holocaust in 1940, it's the Inquisition, it's everything in history.

EW: It is everything. The question, of course, is already in the Bible with Adam and Eve. Adam didn't do anything wrong. Why did he suffer? What was his sin? He obeyed his wife. He didn't touch the fruit. If anyone is guilty, it's Eve, not Adam. Furthermore, what happened? They had a choice between tasting from the tree of knowledge or the tree of life. Had they chosen from the tree of life, they would have been immortal. But they chose the tree of knowledge: be man rather than gods—immortal. Why should they suffer?

The problem is there and the problem of suffering cannot be solved because it's either/or. Either you suffer too and in that case you cannot ask the question and dissociate yourself from it or you don't suffer and then you have no questions—or you have no right to ask questions. What we try to do is to establish certain degrees. I have the right to answer questions with regard to my suffering, maybe even accept it. I have the right to transcend it and say, "Well, that's the will of God." But I have no right to pass by your suffering. If I see someone suffer I cannot say it's God's will.

HJC: Why, then, don't the Jews hate more?

EW: It would be so easy. If we were to hate everyone who made us suffer, we would become a people full of hate. Who didn't persecute us in history? Even God made us suffer. I think this is our defiance; we cannot hate. We don't want to hate because that would be to give in to the enemy. If we were to answer with hate, it would reduce the whole experience to a cheap anecdote. When we answer to hate not with hate, not with love either—we are not Christians—but with an affirmation of life and go on and fight hate, but fight it without hate, simply by shaping our own destiny, telling our tale and becoming the example, then it creates some meaning which transcends the present, the routine. Otherwise, it's silly.

Why should the Jewish people want to stay alive if its existence was nothing but an episode limited to mediocrity, hate-love, persecution-hate? We don't accept that purpose. We try to elevate it. By refusing the option of hate I think we elevate our history to a quasi-theological level.

HJC: At one point you mentioned a real problem is not hate but vengeance.

EW: Yes, because the context is the survivor. We are all survivors, you as much as I. Anyone who is alive is a survivor, especially today, some more than others. We Jews today are more survivors than the others, especially those of my generation. Each of us carries a long procession of ghosts, of people whom we have known. May we make decisions in their name? Do we have the right to make a philosophy, an idea, or even a tale with their struggle, their silence, with their deaths? Maybe they did want us to hate, at least for a while. Maybe they did want us to become avengers.

Strange: all the fighters in the ghettos and the camps, all those who resisted, the rebels, they believed in vengeance and their testament was the testament of vengeance. They said, "Avenge our blood!" You find these words in all the chronicles, on all the walls in all the ghettos and in all the prison cellars— "Avenge our blood!" That was one mesage that they left us: to avenge. Yet, we didn't do it. We didn't do it because as Jews we don't believe in vengeance.

Our past, our history, was there to prevent us from becoming bloodthirsty. We cannot. At the same time we ask ourselves, "Perhaps we were wrong in not obeying the last will of some of these victims. Are we worthy of their message? Are we to decide how to avenge their deaths?" I believe that vengeance is silly, stupid. Jewish survival, continuation and continuity, Israel today and the Jewish awakening in Russia and everywhere, *this* is the answer to, or *an* answer to what happened —I don't see it as vengeance. I don't believe in vengeance.

Remember the Book of Esther which we read twice a year

on Purim? God's name is not mentioned in that book. Not once. And the Talmud is wondering why? The answer, I believe, is at the end of the book where we are told that Jews, for a day or two, became avengers. God, I believe, says, "If this is so, my place is not there." God may be the God of vengeance, but not man. And yet, we are here and alive, talking and thinking and creating. But the victims? *They* are *there*, dead.

HJC: But I remember the story you tell, I guess it was during the Six Day War, where the conquering Jewish Army comes across an Arab woman having a baby and you were proud, you said, that the doctor took care of the woman.

EW: I was proud of the doctor; I was proud of that commander. Proud that they did not think in terms of hate, that they remained human even in the middle of battles. That makes the greatness of Israel, the great human dimension, the Messianic dimension, of Israel.

HJC: What about the Arab situation?

EW: It's a double tragedy. I understand the Arab tragedy. Unfortunately we are also traumatized by what has happened. Although I don't like to make comparisons, our trauma is deeper, probably, older than any other trauma. We did not conduct ourselves as occupiers or as killers. Although they are victims, they are not victims as the Jews used to be. There are grades; there are differences. If the Arabs had accepted, in 1947, the partition and if they had not been induced . . . I won't even go into the question of whose fault it was, but if they had not been educated to hate the Jewish people so much, for more than a generation, I would believe that it would be possible today to bring back most of the Arabs who want to come back and to integrate them in Israel.

Unfortunately, now, having read their statements and having read everything that's available in every language I can read—and I read some languages—remembering the '67 War, I believe that to bring back the Arabs to Israel today would mean sooner or later the end of Israel. That is their avowed purpose: they want to destroy Israel. They say it today; the Al Fatah claims it openly.

Because we are a traumatized generation, with all my sympathy—my feeling, my compassion for the Arabs—I am traumatized as a Jew first. We cannot afford the destruction of Israel. It would be the end of the Jewish people. Let the Arabs make peace and many of us would do whatever we can to compensate them for their homes in Israel and resettle them. It's a situation which only can harm both the Arabs and the Jews—and the entire world. It's too dangerous. I think the entire world is in danger because of that situation.

But the solution is no longer and never has been to bring back the refugees to Israel. It could have been possible in the beginning if it hadn't been for the systematic education in Palestinian schools. Read their books; know how the Arabs study mathematics in their elementary schools: you kill six Jews and you kill eight more. How many have you killed? With such an education it's impossible, impossible even to assume that you can have an integrated population between Arabs and Jews.

HJC: I taught foreign students for a number of years and particularly was responsible for students from Saudi Arabia. Every week they received the hate literature from home.

EW: I know, I read it. It hits me again and again. I would so much have preferred to show that we are capable of achieving co-existence.

HJC: Many of the individual students themselves, privately, would not be too sympathetic with their governments' positions. But publicly. . . .

EW: In that case, whom can you trust? What is at stake is not Israel alone but the Jewish people. Once you have this perspective, you cannot but worry.

HJC: I remember that one of the difficult things was that they were here, as students, during the Six Day War and read *Time* magazine and all the jokes about the Arab army—all the jokes about Arabs in particular—and were humiliated. That kind of thing can't help either.

EW: It's getting worse and worse. What could Israel do during the Six Day War? Not win? If they had lost, we know that they would have been killed to the last. They said it; Ahmed Shukeiry said it; they all said it; Nasser said it. Simply reread their speeches of 1967. Israel had to win. Israel won and the

Arabs were humiliated again. It's a vicious circle and we are at a loss to know what to do.

"No matter where you touch a Jew you find a wound," one woman told Nikos Kazantzakis. The truth of this is transmitted in Wiesel's characters, and his life, just as this truth is rendered by Wiesel's friend Andre Schwarz-Bart in *The Last Of The Just.*

The fact is Elie Wiesel is four thousand years old.

In a period when most of us are fanatically refusing to recognize our aging, when make-up and face lifts and similar lies keep others—and more importantly keep ourselves—from a truth about ourselves, Wiesel and his people (fictional as well as many, many real Jews) assume a more important identity: that of their whole selves. Jung talks about the collective unconscious in which we are inheritors of the past. Christianity has its own notion of psychic interaction (to use an inadequate description) in the idea of the mystical body of Christ. Teilhard's concept of the noosphere, too, should be mentioned in this discussion.

What marks Wiesel, what marks his father as we know him through *Night,* and Michael in *The Town Beyond The Wall,* also the narrator in *The Accident,* clearly Gavriel in *The Gates of the Forest,* even David in *Dawn,* is their willing assumption of their past, which includes their wounds. Judaism and Jews survive precisely because they know where they came from and, thus, somehow understand something about where they are going. This implies, of course, knowing who they are in the present.

Anyone who studies contemporary poetry can draw some conclusions concerning national and international situations that have a bearing here. Scandinavian writing in particular, and European poetry in general, is very pessimistic. Why not? Their Western political and religious dominance is crumbling and clearly their spirit is, too, as reflected in their poetry. The same is true in Japan and, of course, the United States as well. It would be impossible to take a Walt Whitman seriously today, singing America. College sophomores now find Whitman embarrassing to read; his emotion, at first blush, seems to lack the notion of Eliot's objective correlative or Hopkins' inscape. Only South American poetry, to some degree, and African, in major proportion, are literatures of optimistic self-comprehension, if we can generalize about such things. Read George Awoonor-Williams (Ghana), Kwesi Brew (Ghana), Roland Tombehai Dempster (Liberia), Tsagaye Gabre Medhen (Ethiopia), Valente Malagatana (Mozambique), and, of course, Leopold Sedar Senghor (Senegal) for illustration of the point.

Senghor, for example, even as a Catholic, knows precisely who he is as an African and as a Black. Each of these authors has assumed his past and is able to better know his present. It is as if each, as with Wiesel and his characters, has absorbed the Kazantakis of *The Saviours Of God*, his spiritual exercises, wherein he teaches:

> "Your first duty, in completing your service to your race, is to feel within you all your ancestors. Your second duty is to throw light on their onrush and to continue their work. Your third duty is to pass on to your son the great mandate to surpass you."

Who am I, the contemporary troubled Indian in the United States asks, if not the river made up of the tributaries of my ancestors, flowing into the ocean of my successors.

The Jew, then, can clearly be seen as a metaphor for man. What a Jew suffers, all men suffer. What is done to Jews is done to all men. What we did at Auschwitz, we

070020

did to ourselves. In a television conversation several years before the interview recorded in this book took place, I asked Wiesel this question: "This has to be carefully phrased because it could seem an irreverent question, and I don't mean it that way, but is there some sense in which it could be said that those who perished in this Holocaust triumphed and their executioners were defeated?"

Here is Wiesel's reply:
"No. I think the word 'triumph,' unfortunately, does not apply to anything relevant to the Holocaust. There was no triumph. I think Man was defeated there."

Earlier in that same talk, Wiesel had noted the high number of practicing Christians who participated in the massacres of Jewish people and he had observed that, "The sincere Christian knows that what died in Auschwitz was not the Jewish people but Christianity." We killed ourselves.

So, there could be no Hiroshima without Auschwitz, Buchenwald, Dachau, Treblinka, Birkenau, Belsen, Mauthausen, Belzec, Majdanek, Ponar, Sobibor. . . . The step from personal to impersonal Holocaust is a sane, logical transition but the latter cannot precede the former. When faced with the question of the non-rebellion of Jews in concentration camps, Wiesel returns another question: "Why didn't the killers rebel?"

They did, Elie Wiesel, they did. We now kill in a different way. Not myriads of people but megacorpses. Not face to face but from above, far above and soon, by button, from far away horizontally, also. The killing will be clean, like the state's death penalty, carried out in our name; the executions will be effected with only the victims present.

Chaim Kaplan's question is rendered meaningless. In his *Scroll Of Agony*, a Warsaw diary discovered after his own annihilation, he noted that as soon as he arrived at his camp, a torturer—a stranger to him—began beating Kaplan viciously. "How can he hate me?" Kaplan wondered, "He doesn't even know me." (A reversal of Thomas Aquinas who said we cannot love what we do not know. But hate. . . ?) Kaplan's question is superfluous now because the long distance killing can be done unemotionally. My Lai, in Vietnam, might be historically important because it might be the last massacre of its kind—personal, angry, insane. From now on they may be impersonal, unimpassioned and above all, sane.

I think one of the questions Wiesel implies is, do we have something more in store for Jews?

3 / ג

*B*ut they surprised us. Soviet Jewish youth has remained Jewish to a degree beyond anything we could possibly have expected.

I do not know where all these young people came from. They didn't tell me, although I asked. Perhaps there is no one answer, but tens of thousands that are all the same. No matter —they came.

Who sent them? Who persuaded them to come running to spend a Jewish holiday in a Jewish atmosphere and in accordance with traditional Jewish custom? Who told them when and where and why? I was not able to discover. Perhaps they knew but preferred not to say in public. Fine. Let them preserve their secret. All that matters is that they have one and that they came.

Still, there is something strange about it. Tens of thousands of youngsters emerge from nowhere at a specified time and place. Someone had to organize and direct them; someone had to make the contacts, maintain the necessary spirit, and inform them of the date and time. Who made all the preparations? Who breathed the spark into a flame? I didn't ask; they wouldn't have answered. Perhaps it is better for me not to know.

They came in droves. From near and far, from downtown and the suburbs, from the university and from the factories, from school dormitories and from the Komsomal club. They came in groups; they came alone. But once here, they became a single body, voicing a song of praise to the Jewish people and its will to live.

How many were there? Ten thousand? Twenty thousand? More. About thirty thousand. The crush was worse than it had been inside the synagogue. They filled the whole street, spilled over into courtyards, dancing and singing. They seemed to hover in mid air, Chagall-like, floating above the mass of shadows and colors below, above time, climbing a Jacob's ladder that reached to the heavens, if not higher.

Tomorrow they would descend and scatter, disappear into the innermost parts of Moscow, not to be heard from for another year. But they would return and bring more with them. The line will never break; one who has come will always return.

They sang and danced, I walked among them like a sleepwalker, stunned by what I saw and heard, half disbelieving my own senses. I had known they would celebrate, but not that their celebration would be so genuine and so deeply Jewish.

They sang and danced, talked among themselves or with strangers. They were borne along on a crest that seemed incapable of breaking. Their faces reflected a special radiance, their eyes the age-old flame that burned in the house of their ancestors—to which they seemed finally to have returned.

(*The Jews of Silence,* pp. 58-60.)

HJC: In your conversation with Frank Reynolds you mentioned you were pessimistic about mankind but optimistic about the Jewish people. Would you elaborate on that?

EW: I read newspapers. I see what's happening. We are becoming more and more dehumanized. Take, for instance, today—there are men going to the moon; while we are talking, men are going to the moon! How many people in the streets stop to look up to the sky? How many people remember? It has become such a routine. People aren't interested. Man goes to the moon and here below we are indifferent.

Furthermore, deep down, I believe that one day mankind will have to pay for Auschwitz. If I believe in punishment—and I believe in punishment more than in reward—then the punishment will be total, just as Auschwitz meant total crime. Therefore, I am pessimistic.

If I'm optimistic it's because I believe that we, as Jews still can save mankind. This is the irony of history—we who suffered most will, once again, try to bring more blessings and save more people from enduring our fate, the fate that those very people had imposed upon us.

HJC: It must clearly disappoint you, then, to say as you do in your lectures, that American Jewishness does not have total consciousness; American Jews do not have total consciousness of their Jewishness.

EW: I am usually critical of American leadership, of the Jewish leadership too in America. Sometimes I'm too critcal when I speak to Jews but that is because I always include myself in the criticism. I never say "you," I say "we." It is true. I think the leadership is not up to its standards.

The young people, on the other hand, are waiting. The young Jews are good and they want to learn, they want to know. They are hungry. The leadership is too political. Maybe, again, it has to do with the Holocaust. So much was lost and so many occasions were missed; so many opportunities were ignored because of the weak leadership then. Even now we are paying the price for it. Yet, I believe that one day some young leadership will emerge, here too, and bring back to our community its conscience, its consciousness, its awareness, its responsibilities.

HJC: When I saw you in St. Louis, after you finished speaking to an essentially Jewish group, I, as an outsider, could get the feeling —I'm asking you to help me evaluate this—of that young leadership being there: the spontaneous dancing that erupted when you finished. The joy that was evident and the concern obvious among the young students.

EW: We have magnificent young people everywhere. They staged a spiritual revolution for it's not a political revolution that is taking place in Russia now among all the young Jews who want to rebecome Jewish and come to Israel—it's a spiritual revolution. This revolution is conducted and initiated only by young people, by the grandchildren of Stalin's victims, the grandchildren of sworn Communists: Yakir, Markish—these were all great Communists, the very first rank. The grandchildren want to return to their people. They now testify that the old dream of universalism, by doing away with Jewishness, is a lost dream, a false dream. They return to their origins. Well, if the young people in Russia surprised us so beautifully, I don't think we have the right to doubt the young people in America.

In general, young Jews today are aware, are concerned with values. They were among the first to fight against the war in Vietnam and they were the first to fight for civil rights. These are good youngsters, good students. They want to know the meaning of life again. What is it all about? To be Jewish? To be human? To be alive? To be part of a society? The problem is not the youth, the problem is the leadership. And that applies not only to the Jewish people, it applies to everyone. Do you know of any voice—a moral voice—that would command authority today saying, "Follow me," and people would follow?

HJC: You are sometimes critical of the Jews but that isn't your only position and you do have a lot of exposure to American Jews, and not only American Jews but world Jews. How are you received by Jews? How is your work received?

EW: There were many stages. I think I am being received now because I don't belong to any sects. I see myself as belonging to the entire community of Israel. When I come to Reform Jews I speak about Orthodox Jews; when I come to Orthodox Jews I speak about Reform Jews. I try to build the bridge. If I am received now, it's also because I was received beforehand by the non-Jewish world which is rather sad to say for a Jew. Once the non-Jewish world listened to and read me, the Jews too began reading my work.

The fact is that, practically, I owe Francois Mauriac my career. He was a Christian and we were very close friends. Had it not been for Mauriac, I would have become or remained an obscure writer, a journalist.

I think Jews listen now because the young people listen and I feel responsible for the young people. I want to transmit to them certain experiences that I had lived. They know that through me they, the leaders, have a vehicle of communication to their own young people.

Mainly, my position in the Jewish community is really the position of a witness from within and defender from without. This goes, of course, along with my ideas about the duties and the privileges of a storyteller—of a writer. From the inside, from within the community, I am critical. If Jews are criticized or attacked from the outside, then I try to defend them. What I try to do (it's very hard) is to reconcile the two attitudes: not to be too strong, too sharp, too critical when I am inside and not to be a liar on the outside.

HJC: It was in a Catholic magazine that I discovered you—a now defunct magazine, *Jubilee*.

EW: I remember. They carried the first *Night* excerpts. You see, it's true. Even in America I had to be discovered first by the non-Jewish public; the Jews followed. Maybe it's a sense of insecurity on the part of the Jews: they don't trust their own judgment. Even more so, I think it has to do with a diaspora reflex.

We never had too much consideration for the writer. A writer was a kind of what we call in Hebrew, a *batlan*, someone with nothing else to do; he wrote books. To write books is not a real profession; it cannot mean success. A scholar, yes, but writing books? Who writes books? Someone who has nothing else to do. Today, in America, it's different because in America literature has become big business. One can be a successful writer; one can even become a millionaire if one is eager and lucky. I am not.

The danger, naturally, is that once it happens, the successful Jewish writer may be tempted to cater to the non-Jewish world which would lift him up even higher and thus have even greater impact on the Jewish community. This is the danger that one must overcome. One must write out of one's own experience, out of one's own identity. One must cater to no one; one must remain truthful. If one is read, it's good; if one is not read, it's too bad. But that should not influence the writer.

HJC: Can Jews and Christians have a meeting ground after Asuchwitz?

EW: They can because they should. But before that meeting can take place, certain words must be said. I think Jews must say, first, certain words which hurt Christians—that Auschwitz would not have been possible without Christianity. John XXIII understood this. The fact that Hitler was never excommunicated; the fact that, I think, over twenty percent of the S.S. killers were practicing Christians; the fact that Pius XII never spoke up means that Christianity's role, or the Christian Church's role—both Protestant and Catholic—was so dominant in the fact that so many Jews could have been killed. All that has to be said. I think the Christians must recognize it as John XXIII did.

Once all this has been articulated, I think there can be a meeting ground, provided one does not try to convert the other. Conversion is not a solution; authenticity is the solution. If the Christians give up their dream to convert Israel (Israel never tried to convert the Church) then I'm sure we can find some common ground.

HJC: Historically, has the role of the Christian been that of persecutor?

EW: For many centuries the Christian defined himself by the suffering he imposed on the Jew. The more the Jew suffered, the better a Christian was. Theologically, the Christian saw that he was *the* Jew, the true Jew; the true Israel was the Church. The others had to suffer for not becoming part of the new concept of Judaism. Despite that suffering, I think a ground can and should be found in honesty, without hidden thoughts, without

34

rancor. These ideas must be explored; these truths must be confessed—on both sides.

HJC: George Bernanos may have begun a kind of recognition. He said Buchenwald was not a chance phenomenon but the culminating abcess collecting pus.

EW: So did many others in France. Mauriac was sensitive to the problem. We became so close because of his recognition of Christian responsibility. He understood the part of the Vatican and he was the first to come out against Pius XII. It wasn't Rolf Hochhuth, it was Mauriac.

But then, French literature was influenced by Christianity and the entire right wing had the courage to accept, after the war, the fact that it was anti-Semitic before the war. They grew up with anti-Semitism. Great writers were anti-Semites. Gide himself once recognized that he used to be anti-Semitic—without knowing it, without wanting it. This honest approach must be made first. This means a return to honesty and saying, "Yes, we were guilty; we were wrong. Not directly because we didn't participate in the crimes. But as Christians, the Christian past in us made us guilty." If and when it is acknowledged, I think something can be done; something important can be undertaken and achieved.

HJC: So you are not automatically pessimistic about the future of Christianity?

EW: If it goes the way it has then, of course, I am pessimistic. But the Christians themselves are more pessimistic than I. The crises that occur now within Christianity are unprecedented. I think these young forces within Christianity, the serious, sincere attempt being made by some young Christian theologians and teachers, must be pursued—of having a re-evaluation of Christianity in terms of conscience, morality and its relationship to the Jewish people. Once it is done, once these young forces prevail, we can go on. Then I am an optimist.

HJC: Otherwise we can have Auschwitz again?

EW: Not Auschwitz again for the Jewish people but for the entire world. I don't believe there can be another Holocaust for the Jewish people so soon. It's impossible. The event is unique and because of that, it cannot be repeated. I believe, with fear, that if there should be another Holocaust it will be a universal Holocaust. Some madman, some insane criminal, will seize power somewhere in a small nation, or a big nation, and he will push the button. The chain reaction will be of such terror that the world will go to pieces. Mankind will come to the end of its road.

HJC: It seems—I will put this in simplistic terms—but in one sense it seems all we have to do is remember. And we are not remembering, we are forgetting.

EW: Do we forget? Of course we forget. There is a movement towards forgetfulness. I will give you an example. In my own class, which is a good class, I asked my students, "Who is Bormann?" because the newspapers recently spoke about Bormann. I think two out of a hundred knew. I asked, "Who was Hess?" Nobody knew. Eichmann? Some knew but some didn't. In Israel over 1200 high school students were asked similar questions and they showed abysmal ignorance. People in general want to forget because it was too horrible, too evil, too sad, too morbid.

Take society. Germany today is the victorious power, the strongest nation in Europe, without any complexes. We know Brandt got the Nobel Peace Prize and it was clear everywhere that he got it for Germany, not for himself. The irony, as you yourself have noted, immediately afterwards it was Heinrich Böll. Clearly, it was supposed to be a German year, as they call it in Stockholm. The whole world is catering now to Germany and Germany today has been accepted again as a moral nation. Not only as a moral nation but *the* moral nation on earth which is sad. I think Brandt is an honest person but after all, this is the generation of the victims and the generation of the hangmen and some are still alive. I would have believed that something should have been done to mark the existence or the subsistence of these two generations. It wasn't done. There are still people who remember among the victims. There are still people who remember among the hangmen, the executioners. The world behaves as if the last executioner and the last victim had died. No, we don't remember and because we don't I'm afraid something will happen.

HJC: There's a kind of hideous symbolism in what happened at the Olympic Games happening in Munich.

36

EW: It had to happen in Munich, the way it happened. I was shocked, horrified, that when one day after the massacre the President of the Olympic Games, Avery Brundage, in his speech said, "Well, we are sad and so forth, but the games will continue tomorrow," and 80,000 people began applauding. There was such a thunder of applause. Well, really! Eleven victims and the applause! It was unbelievable. Later on, when the Arabs seized a German airplane, the Germans were glad to get rid of the three terrorists and they sent them back to Libya where they were welcomed as heroes. So, why shouldn't it continue? Somebody is writing a certain script but we cannot read it. We cannot decipher the code.

HJC: In *One Generation After*, you say there's no possible salvation for Germans outside of their relationship with Jews.

EW: If the Germans want to atone they can; I don't accuse any young German, of course. They are, to me, as innocent as any other human being can be. But the young German, because of what he is, because of his parents, must take a position with regard to the Jews. Just as I must take a position. We are linked somehow together, mysteriously, in the same destiny, the same obsessions. So, I believe the young Germans too, not only the old ones, must take positions and define their existence with regard to the Jewish people. Then if the choice is a good one, there is cause for celebration. There is a chance for understanding.

HJC: Once, on a television network program, I saw two comedians, one Jewish, joking about Bormann, having him over for a party or something like that.

EW: How can you speak of taste? I don't know how you felt. How can one joke about these things? On the other hand, I read that Günther Grass was asked whether he believed a museum should be built in Auschwitz and he said, "No, a circus," because there was something farcical about it. The whole Holocaust had a farcical aspect. That is my haunting fear—maybe it was a farce, it wasn't even a tragedy. Tragedy for us but not in other terms. It was a farce. Laughter. Laughter.

Some years ago, in Frankfurt, they had a trial of the Auschwitz S.S. killers. I remember I read the proceedings. The indicted, the defendants, listened to witnesses and they couldn't resist laughing. They went on laughing *in the courtroom*. These murderers went on laughing and I found it symbolic, instructive.

HJC: You attended the Eichmann trial; you mention that somewhere.

EW: Yes. Well, he didn't laugh.

HJC: No. But he was more frightening under glass than when you saw him as a child.

EW: Yes, because I suddenly realized that evil doesn't even have to be expressed. Evil is evil. Although he was defenseless in the glass booth, he was frightening.

HJC: You mentioned the lady who would not attend the trial because she didn't want to be seen by him.

EW: She didn't want to have any link, any connection with him; she didn't want her image to be taken away by him. What does it mean really? It means that he was a human being. The frightening aspect of the Holocaust is that even the killers were human. Someone—psychologists—did research on that and concluded that the killers didn't have their moral sense impaired. They still knew what was good and what was evil. Their sense of reality was impaired.

When they killed Jews they didn't feel bad; they didn't feel they were committing any evil deed. To them a Jew had no reality, no life; he was not a human being. These same killers knew they had to be kind with children, their own children, only their perception of reality was distorted. Yet they were human, which is frightening, because it leads to other questions. Are we sure that these killers were the only ones who were killers? Are we sure that someone else who didn't have the opportunity to go that far—to that extent—couldn't have become an Eichmann or a Bormann? What shield do we possess to protect us from becoming inhuman?

HJC: The photograph that *The New York Times* ran with a children's review that you did—there's a small child with a look on his face . . . I react just to the *photograph!* How could anybody not react to the *reality*?

EW: It's familiarity, you know. Now even more than ever when I have a son, I think about it and I'm honest enough—cruel enough to myself—to find myself thinking, "Well, it could have been him."

When you think that one million children . . . *one million children* . . . were killed, massacred, burned alive. . . . These children were even more victim than the others. The grownups —the Germans employed methods to fool them, to kill them without their being aware of it. But the children—they played with them as targets and they threw them in the air and shot them. Sometimes they tore a child, a baby, away from his mother and tore him to pieces alive. Sometimes, in 1944, they threw them in flames, alive.

When I saw it I was convinced that it wasn't true and I recorded it almost as a nightmare. Then I found the documents, the corroboration and it was true. They had so many killings to do in those days—the Hungarian Jews, my Jews— that they did burn them alive. You imagine one million children. . . .

HJC: You talked earlier of the world behaving as if the last executioner was gone, in a sense had paid. As I recall, Martin Buber was against executing Eichmann because—I believe these were his reasons—the world would then say, "Well, the crime has been atoned for." How do you feel about that? Do you think Eichmann should have been executed? He is the only person executed in all of Israel for a crime.

EW: I'm, in general, against capital punishment. With regard to Eichmann, I prefer to pass on that. I prefer not to give a statement because Israel is involved. I have no right to decide for Israel. But I accept whatever Israel does and I accept that it does it in my name.

There is a beautiful Hasidic story about a great Rebbe, of whom I speak in *Souls On Fire*, who traveled by train one day. His traveling companion was a rich man who didn't know who the Rebbe was so he behaved arrogantly. When they reached the destination, the Rebbe was received with great honors and the rich man, aware suddenly of whom he insulted, came to ask forgiveness. The Rebbe said, "I cannot forgive you." The rich man pleaded with him, crying, imploring him, "Please forgive me! I didn't know who you were." The Rebbe said, "Listen, you didn't insult *me*. You didn't know who I was. You insulted a poor beggar. So, go to all the poor beggars; let them forgive you."

The same applied to Eichmann. How can I really speak on behalf of those whom he killed? Only they could decide what to do with Eichmann. What Israel does—maybe I'm too weak and too inhibited and also too Jewish to criticize or to say one way or another—what Israel does, Israel does. And does it for me.

HJC: Do you think, 'though, there was the "practical effect" on the world of taking the burden of guilt off some shoulders?

EW: No. Nobody really remembered. I think Eichmann's *trial* was important. It made people read and reflect. People wanted to know then why certain things happened and in what manner. I don't think that because of Eichmann's removal from the scene —his physical removal—the people in the world felt less the burden of guilt than before.

As I prepare this manuscript for publication, the *National Catholic Reporter*, a totally lay-edited newspaper, breaks a tragic story about an unpublished papal encyclical letter on anti-Semitism, a letter which, had it been circulated, might have had an immense effect on the prosecution and persecutions of World War II. Pope Pius XI commissioned a U.S. Jesuit priest, John LaFarge, to write an encyclical for the Pope, attacking racism and anti-Semitism. The request was made in June, 1938, a full fifteen months before the outbreak of the Second World War. Through a series of apparently Machiavellian machinations, the message never got into print. After examining the evidence, an editorial writer for the *National Catholic Reporter* indicated that, "Considering all this, we must conclude that the publication of the encyclical draft at the time it was written may have saved hundreds of thousands, perhaps millions, of lives."

I wish I could say the story is incredible. But I have read Church history and it is all *too* believable. Father La-

Farge wrote *Humani Generis Unitas (The Unity Of The Human Race)* as requested but apparently his Jesuit Superior General, a Polish count, Father Wlodimir Ledochowski, withheld the completed manuscript from the Pope for what *NCR* concluded were "political reasons." Pius XI's death the following February doomed the anti-Semitic declaration to limbo. (Cardinal Jean Tisserant, a close associate of the Pope, claimed that Pius XI was poisoned by a physician, Dr. Francesco Petacci, whose daughter Clara was Mussolini's mistress. The Pope died on the eve of a scheduled speech to Italian bishops which was to have been an attack on Fascism.) When the successor Pope, Pius XII, published his first encyclical—using the title of LaFarge's work—the sections on racism and anti-Semitism were not included. Here is Jim Castelli's account as it appears in the *NCR*:

> The anti-Semitism section entitled, "The Jews and Anti-Semitism (Religious Separation)" directly follows the racism section. It begins by saying, "It becomes clear that the struggle for racial purity ends by being uniquely the struggle against Jews."

The encyclical draft said contemporary anti-Semitism has historical roots:

> "Save for the systematic cruelty, this struggle, in true motives and methods, is no different from persecutions everywhere carried out against the Jews from antiquity. These persecutions have been censured by the Holy See on more than one occasion, but especially when they have worn the mantle of Christianity."

The following paragraphs described the "actual persecution of the Jews":

> "As a result of such a persecution, millions of persons are deprived of the most elementary rights and

privileges of citizens in the very land of their birth. Denied legal protection against violence and robbery, exposed to every form of insult and public degradation, innocent people are treated as criminals though they have circumspectly obeyed the law of their native land.

"Even those who in time of war fought bravely for their country are treated as traitors, and the children of those who laid down their lives in their country's behalf are branded as outlaws by the very fact of their parentage. The values of patriotism, so loudly invoked for the benefit of one class of citizens, are ridiculed when invoked for others who come under the racial ban.

"In the case of the Jews, this flagrant denial of human rights sends many thousands of helpless persons out over the face of the earth without any resources. . . ."

There's more, but it is difficult to continue. Another Catholic lay publication, the magazine *Commonweal*, editorialized about the scandal: ". . . there is no evading the past; it is true that many Christians were all-too-ready to co-operate in the persecution of the Jews, and it is this fact, even more than the silence of Pius XII, that stains the collective conscience of Christians. History is dealing harshly with Pius XII on this issue and rightly so, but on this side of the Atlantic as well as the other he was not alone in keeping silence."

So, while Elie Wiesel can write a book and lecture about *The Jews Of Silence*, a silence in a double sense—one magnificent and one shameful—we can only write of *The Christians of Silence* in a single sense. What is a tragedy for Jews in time—their surrender by their brothers—is a tragedy for eternity for Christians. . . .

A slight individual reparation was made to Wiesel by Francois Mauriac, whose Foreword to *Night* may be seen as a personal encyclical from a Christian to a Jew. The French novelist, who was to win the Nobel Prize, wrote of the lambs he had seen being carted to slaughter and how young (was he ever a youth?) Elie Wiesel had to be to be among them. The Foreward contains the words Mauriac wished he had spoken to Wiesel at their first meeting but could not: "This is what I should have told this Jewish child. But I could only embrace him, weeping." Mauriac's own book of reflections on the life of Christ, *The Son of Man*, is dedicated:

TO
Elie Wiesel
Who was a crucified Jewish child.
His friend
F. M.

That too is an encyclical, in form as well as content.

4 / ר

Q. *In your books, the notion of silence plays an important role.
Characters in your novels as-
sume silence for long periods. Could you tell us a little bit
about your ideas on this silence?*

A. *I have many obsessions, as you know. There are certain
key sentences or key expressions in my mythology, in my universe. One of them is the eyes. The other one is silence. Why?
Because of my upbringing. As a child I studied the Talmud,
and also mysticism. My master was a mystic. And silence, in
mysticism, is extremely important; it's the essential. What you
don't say carries weight. For instance, I wondered many times:
within our tradition we know what God said at Sinai. But there
are certain silences between word and word. How was this silence transmitted? This is the silence that I tried to put in my*

work, and I tried to link it to that silence, the silence of Sinai. There is a healthy silence, Sinai, and an unhealthy silence, that of chaos before Creation. There is a political silence which is criminal: today to be silent when so many injustices are being performed and perpetuated—in Russia against the Jews; in Vietnam against the Vietnamese; in all kinds of countries against minorities. To be silent today is criminal.

On the other hand, there is a different silence which is penetrated, inspired. When you want to say something and you don't say it, it is still there. When I hear a beautiful trio by Beethoven or Mozart, I feel gratitude towards Beethoven and Mozart, and I keep quiet, and then I feel that I share, I participate in the playing with my silence. So silence is, of course, a universe of silence. And you can say about it what you can say about life and about death and about God. And the totality of what you say will not make up completely what there is to be said about it.

(*U.S. Catholic/Jubilee,* September, 1971, p. 30.)

HJC: We talked about silence earlier. I'd like to get back to that subject. First of all: Kazantzakis says, "Silence is the tongue of angels." I would guess you've read a lot of Kazantzakis.

EW: Yes. He's a very great writer. I feel a kind of communion with his writing, with his heroes. He was a great friend of the Jews. In the '20's or the '30's he even had a Jewish friend whom I know, an old poetess. She told him things Jewish to such an extent that he learned Hebrew. He went to Palestine in the '20's. Then in the '30's, when he went to Russia, invited by the government to see the revolution, he came back with a book. He titled the book *Toda Raba,* the name of one of his heroes, an African man. *Toda Raba* sounds very African except that in Hebrew it means "thank you."

He used to fast on Yom Kippur, the Day of Forgiveness. He felt very Jewish. At the same time he was, like Mauriac, deeply taken with the Christ.

But I don't agree with his definition. Silence is not the

tongue of angels. Silence can be only the tongue of man because angels sing. In our tradition, especially, the angels sing and some sing only one song and then they die. The difference between men and angels is that angels have only one task to perform and they die; man has more than one task to perform and in more ways than one.

HJC: I'm very unhappy when I see Kazantzakis referred to as a minor writer. He has meant a great deal to me personally and I guess I transfer that into major writer status.

EW: He is a major writer. Who says that he is a minor writer?

HJC: I've read that in several critics of Greek literature.

EW: It's strange; he was not too popular with the Greeks.

HJC: Yes. In fact, he was unwelcome in his country for a while.

EW: He was popular in France and in America but not in Greece. I wonder why? Maybe because they feel that he romanticized Crete and Greece too much. I don't know. I think he was one of the major writers of this generation.

HJC: He has a whole book built around a passion play.

EW: Oh, beautiful; *Christ Recrucified.*

HJC: You have a similar kind of scene, revolving around Judas, in *The Gates Of The Forest.*

EW: I needed a literary frame, to say certain things about our attitude toward Christianity. Why did I do that? Because for two thousand years we ignored Christianity and I think it was wrong to do so. We did that willingly. The moment they became heretics, from our point of view, the Jewish nation and religion expelled or excommunicated the heretics and ignored them. The result was bad. From time to time we had pogroms in the street but somehow, the Talmudic scholars three steps away were sitting and studying Talmud as if nothing happened. They were so obtuse to Christian history, as if it didn't exist. It was easier maybe, or maybe it was a good solution, to go on living. I think we should open and accept that it exists. We should come to terms with its existence and see what we are going to do with it.

But I had to place it in our contemporary framework and say what we feel about it. Therefore, I rehabilitated Judas in that play, in that novel. Also, I wanted to say what we really felt. We felt that whether Christ himself was innocent or not is a matter for Christians to decide. Whether he was the Christ is for Christians to decide. As far as the Jews are concerned, he may be retroactively guilty for all the murders and massacres that were done in his name. I believe that the Christians betrayed the Christ more than the Jews did.

I say it also in *The Beggar*, when I come back to it almost in a transition. Shlomo the seer, in *The Beggar*, describes his meeting with Jesus and when he tells him, "Please come back, come back and don't think that you are going to be a benefactor for mankind or for your people; I'm showing you what they are going to do in your name." But then Jesus began crying and he said, "It's too late, too late." I tried then to understand Jesus' tragedy, Jesus' drama, that it's too late. He knew that they were going to misinterpret his teaching and distort it and make it inhuman.

HJC: The meaning of history is often changed by successive generations so that as the meaning of Jesus can be changed, the meaning of Hitler can be changed.

 EW: Then it's up to poets, historians and witnesses to try to keep not the meaning, but at least the experience as alive as possible. We cannot change events but we can change meanings. That's our force. We use it and we abuse it.

HJC: Kazantzakis is attracted to silence, a kind of silence I think of as the Buddhists': truth is beyond names, beyond forms, is incommunicable. Joseph Campbell somewhere says that mythology is the penultimate word but silence is the ultimate word.

 EW: Silence plays a part in every mysticism. Kazantzakis was a mystic. Silence plays a part in Christian mysticism as well. How many orders do you have that are built around silence? Trappist monks and so forth. We too, in Judaism, have in our mystical tradition many currents leading to silence. Silence is enriching. God's voice is heard in silence—true silence—and sometimes *is* silence. We say, for instance, that one way of purifying man is to purify his language, his word. How does one purify it? Through silence. What is prayer if not the entrance of silence into language? What is prayer if not the exclusion of certain words, the protection of others, the creation of a certain zone of silence between one word and another.

HJC: In *One Generation After* you say, and this is the kind of silence

I think you are talking about, "Silence demands to be transmitted."

EW: Yes, that's the end, almost, of the last summing up of the book. As usual I take one sentence and later on build a book on it. The present novel about Moshe the Madman is about this sentence, how to transmit silence and this is the silence I refer to.

HJC: There's a scholar of American literature, Ihab Hassan. . . .

EW: I know him. He wrote a book on The Literature of Silence.

HJC: Yes, *The Dismemberment of Orpheus*. Yes. It's a genre that's being recognized now. Obviously it existed but now it is being ascertained that it is existing. You mention in *The Town Beyond The Wall* that the hero of your story *is* silence.

EW: It is. It's the invisible hero and I try to make him become more and more dominant and visible.

HJC: You mention, in that book, St. Exupery who talks about the silences of the desert.

EW: The different shades of silences. It's inspiring. In general, you can recognize a poet by the way he speaks of silence. I think that every poet, at one time or another, must come to speak about silence.

This is not the ascetic silence that means the withdrawal from language. On the contrary, the emphasis is *on* language; the emphasis is on transmission. Certain words carry their silence with them. They have the weight of silence and you can judge a text: the Biblical text is great and eternal because it has eternal silence in it; the text written in the last century has only one century of silence in it.

HJC: Fifteen years ago I heard John Ciardi, the poet, talk about the meaning of poetry being in what's between words—the time between words.

EW: This is the measurement, the resonance in words, but even more it is the zone between words. We had a Hasidic master who said that when the Messiah will come, man will understand not only the words but also the space between them.

HJC: I want to move to the topic of names. There is a power in naming, isn't there?

EW: Oh yes. After all, Adam named creation to become the master of creation. When we refer to God in our tradition we call him "The Name." Although he is nameless, he is ineffable. We are all descendents of Semites, of Shem, which is "the name." Noah had three sons; one of them was called, "the name." Therefore, the name was so forceful.

HJC: What happens when one person gives another person his name, as in *The Gates Of The Forest*?

EW: He gives him his destiny. He gives him the most precious thing that he has and that he received. Nothing is stranger to a man than his name, said Valery.

In our tradition, again, it is something else. A son gets the name of his father's father. The names go back to the first name, to Adam.

It was very moving when we had our son circumcised. We had a few friends at the home ceremony. You cannot issue and you cannot refuse an invitation to a circumcision. Why not? Because Abraham himself is the host there and the guest of honor is the prophet Elijah. What person has better things, more important things, to do than to respond to an invitation issued by Abraham or the prophet Elijah? So, one is not supposed to reject an invitation to a circumcision and therefore, one is not supposed to invite. If you want someone to come, then you simply tell him, "You know, the ceremony is taking place on. . . ." If he wants to, he comes. On the other hand, for the same reason, one is not supposed even to get an invitation. If anyone wants to be present, he is.

So, we had a few people here, a mixture of Hasidim and rabbis, musicians and professors, some twenty people. The Hasidic rabbi suddenly turned to me and said, "Well, a name has returned." Why? Because whenever I was called to the Torah, I was called Eliezer (my name) son of Shlomo. Now the rabbi says when my son will come we will call him Shlomo, son of Eliezer. My father, when he was called, was Shlomo, son of Eliezer. "Yes," said the rabbi, "A name has returned."

The return of names, the eternity of names, and the destiny of names has always fascinated me. Therefore, I'm very careful with names. I choose names prudently; they always have a certain meaning, a special meaning to me.

HJC: You mention in *The Gates Of The Forest* that one of the obligations the Jews have is to perpetuate a dead man's name.

EW: When our son was born, I thought, "I cannot be the last of the line; I shouldn't be the last of the line. Even if the world is not worth it. But I cannot make a decision on behalf of three thousand years and say it's enough. The name must go on."

We lost so many names—I'm advocating that each Jew should give to his child another name because too many names were lost. So our son is called Shlomo Elisha, the second name for the same reason. We *must* perpetuate these names.

HJC: This is one of the things the Germans could not eradicate, you said.

EW: They tried hard. The *first* thing that they tried to destroy was the names. When they reduced man to a number they took away his name. When they reduced him to an object, they took away his name. An inmate in the camp was not allowed to keep his name.

HJC: It's happened to others, too, hasn't it? It happened to Blacks in the South who were given slave names; they are now rebelling against that. It happened to American Indians when they were processed by the American Army; they were given jokes for names.

EW: Nicknames and jokes. The process and intention are always the same: to reduce man to an object, to reduce man, period. I think nothing can be more denigrating, nothing can be more humiliating, than to take a name away. Names contain more than life. My name goes back to the Bible.

HJC: I want to get into that because the great Black American novelist, Ralph Ellison, has written an essay on the suggestive power of names. His own name is Ralph Waldo Ellison and he talks in that essay of the suggestive impact that that had on him. I want to ask what your name may have meant to you.

EW: My name is Eliezer which was my grandfather's name, which must have been his grandfather's name. It goes back to Abraham's servant. In the Bible Abraham's servant was called Eliezer. When I think of the name, I think of my grandfather whom I did not know. He died as a medic during the First World War; I was given his name. I also think of a Hasidic rabbi called Eliezer of Wishnitz whom I knew. What it means to me mainly is not Eliezer as such, but Eliezer ben Shlomo. Whenever I hear Eliezer ben Shlomo, son of Shlomo, I react. It is the "ben," the son, the connection with the past, the connection with the father.

HJC: You name a number of your characters either Eliezer or variants of that.

EW: Eliezer only once, for the line. Usually it's the variants of "El", meaning God, not Eliezer. The reference is not to me but to God. Every main character or rebbe has such a name to show the part of God in the name. If there had been no part of God in man, there would be no problem, no metaphysical problem —maybe no man, but certainly no problem.

Our problem always involves God. The Christian problem involves death. We fight with the angel. Jacob's fight with the angel still goes on and that's why he got the name "Isra-el." Again, "El", meaning God. He fought with God and vanquished him, says the Bible. In each character I have a mystical part, therefore he is "El-".

HJC: Paul, in the New Testament, in what I think could be generally regarded as a little known section, speaks, I think, rather condescendingly concerning God as still loving the Jews. The Jews are just going through a disobedient phase. But he does say that the Liberator will come from Zion.

EW: Paul, of course, was the architect of the Church. Judaism rejected him and he in turn rejected Judaism—much more than the others, apparently. When he said he would come from Zion, he didn't mean from Jewish Zion; he meant from his Zion, Christian Zion. However, whether he was right or wrong, who are we to decide?

No man can speak on behalf of God. Remember, Kafka used to say man has only one power, to speak *to* God, not *about* God. I think one of the great beauties in Judaism is that we are warned not to speak about God so much. We always speak to him but not about him. It's dangerous, once you start to interpret God's words. I think that's the reason why most prophets were unhappy, tragic characters and most of them died tragically. They too spoke *to* God, *from* God, and they spoke also *about* God. One is not supposed to do that: God

52

should speak directly to man, as he did on Sinai. Sinai is the revelation, the great moment in creation.

HJC: You spoke about the Christian attitude toward death. What is your attitude toward death?

EW: Do you mean my attitude as a Jew or the Jewish attitude versus the Christian attitude?

I believe Christians sanctified death because they sanctified the crucifixion. They believed that with that death their religion was born. We believe that death is impure. There is no holiness in death; a priest cannot enter a cemetery; anyone who touches a corpse is impure. Moses was the holiest and greatest prophet of all while he was alive. The moment he died —impure.

I believe that one should explore the idea that the sanctification of death throughout the ages produced the indifference to death during the Holocaust. For us, death is impure but more importantly, it's a private affair between man and himself. I'll give you an example. We had a great sage called Rabbi Akiba, who was a counterpart to Paul and his contemporary. He too was a martyr. We had then many martyrs of the faith. When a Christian father died as a martyr, he gave speeches, sermons. When Rabbi Akiba went to die, we are told that when he died, that was the hour for a certain prayer: *Shema Yisroel*, Hear O Israel. The great Talmudic scholar, Professor Saul Lieberman, made the point: "Why does the Talmud say that that was a time of a prayer? If it hadn't been for the time, he wouldn't have said it." He didn't prepare speeches, he gave no sermons. He said it because that was the time to say it. Why? Because man doesn't die in public; his death belongs to himself.

One of the things that was difficult for us, for my generation, was to give back to death this private character. During the war you saw death everywhere, you slept with corpses. When death becomes a routine matter, you don't even look. It took some time for all of the survivors to restore that special feeling about death and to give back to it this sacred and anti-sacred, but special, attitude that death conveyed before.

HJC: Old Varady says that men don't reject death, they reject immortality. Modern psychiatry is now discussing the problem of death being psychosomatic—we willing our own deaths, and I found that an interesting objectification there.

EW: The death wish, you mean.

HJC: Yes.

EW: I don't believe in that. It's not Jewish. We don't want to die. Even Moses, we are told in the Talmud, refused to die. He refused to die because death ultimately means a blemish in creation, as a Jewish mystic said. Something is wrong in creation if man dies. Man doesn't want it; man would like to be immortal.

HJC: Yet we die every day, in certain ways.

EW: We die every day. We come closer to death. But as long as we are alive we are immortal. One moment before we die we are still immortal, for that moment.

HJC: I wanted to talk a little bit about your symbols; for example, tears and clouds. Symbols ought not to be explained in one sense and maybe we shouldn't go into that at all. What do you think about that?

EW: Some symbols, because they are symbols, may be explained. The real symbols are not to be decoded. The real secrets will remain secrets in the books—in the tales. Obvious symbols, for instance, "night": whenever I say "night" I mean the Holocaust, that period. "Night" has become a symbol for the Holocaust for obvious reasons. As we have said, a night has descended upon mankind, not only in Europe, but everywhere. Whoever was alive in those days has absorbed parts or fragments of that night. Night enveloped human destiny and human history. Night is a symbol of that period, a frightening symbol. Whenever I try to speak of those nights, I simply say "night."

It is strange but night, before that, would have meant different things: dreams, poetry, waiting for the Messiah, the lamentation over the destruction of the Temple. Night is a poetic image, a romantic one at that. Night had become the opposite of whatever we call creativity and creation. After all, night preceded day; night induces people to love each other, to give birth and life. Ironically, it has become the opposing symbol, anti-life, anti-man, anti-Messiah.

Tears are not really a symbol because when I speak of

tears, I really mean tears. There were so many that were not shed that they could have filled the entire universe and provoked another deluge.

Clouds are symbols, especially in *The Gates Of The Forest*. I see in the clouds all those Jews who left and returned, the only way for them to return was in clouds. For the first time in history so many victims perished and had no cemeteries. Even the cemeteries were locked from them, from us. Heaven became their cemetery; the clouds became their cemetery. In a weird, strange way, it is symbolic, too, because cemeteries are impure and as Jews we should not dwell in cemeteries. . . .

In ancient time, in Judaea, one was not supposed to build a city on cemeteries. Perhaps it is symbolic that those millions and millions of human beings, because they had no cemeteries, the entire world became freely accessible to them and they to us. That means one *can* dwell on their memory without feeling the impurity coming from cemeteries or from death. Hence, one can even speak of them, or not speak of them, but live their tale without feeling morbidity. It's not a morbid tale. No cemeteries, only clouds.

I remember in those winter nights a particular image. It was Hannukah, the holiday commemorating the Maccabeans. We are supposed to light eight candles because the oil in the Temple burned eight days. This commandment, to observe Hannukah, is not among the most important ones. One can very well be a good Jew, even a religious Jew, and not light the candles. Yet, there were Jews in Auschwitz, Buchenwald, everywhere (I have seen some of them) who risked their lives to light candles. I don't know how they managed. They took margarine which they were supposed to eat to keep alive and they melted it. They found some string and somehow they managed to make a Hannukah lamp. . . .

I think they shouldn't have done it because the image that comes to my mind is a horrible image: Auschwitz as its own Hannukah lamp with its six huge chimneys, throwing flames to the clouds. These six chimneys were to me six Hannukah candles. Why six? Because the week suddenly was reduced to six. The seventh day was negated. There was no Sabbath. Mankind has killed its sabbath. What really took place there?

They took a people and turned them into flames and the flames, in turn, turned them into clouds. The only way for the Jews to come back and haunt our memories is as clouds. Whenever I see clouds, I remember them. Here, too, it's ironic because in Scripture the clouds were meant to protect the Jews. In the desert, after the Exodus, there were clouds and they protected the Hebrews. But now they did not protect them. How could they? They *were* the clouds.

HJC: In Scripture, also, the symbol of the covenant was placed in the clouds.

EW: Yes. But then the covenant, maybe, was broken during the Holocaust. There is a Talmudic passage saying the following: there are two holidays linked to miracles. One is Hannukah and one is Purim. Purim is the story of Haman. Haman wanted to kill the Jews. A young girl, Esther, befriended the king, Ahasuerus, and the Jews were saved. Hannukah is also a miracle; a miracle because the Maccabeans rebelled against the Greeks and the assimilationists and the Temple was saved.

What is the question? In the time of Hannukah, what was in danger? Not the physical aspect of the Jewish people, but the spiritual aspect. The Greeks didn't want to kill the Jews, they wanted to convert them, to assimilate them. And yet the Maccabeans fought with weapons. What was the story of Purim? Haman didn't want to convert the Jews; he wanted to kill them. What did Mordechai, Esther's uncle do? He didn't take up arms; he began praying and fasting and he proclaimed the fast.

The Talmud answers: a covenant had been made between God and his people. God said, "I give you the Torah, the law. You observe the law and I shall protect you. You protect my word and I shall defend you." When the law was in danger in the time of Hannukah, the Maccabeans rebelled, physically. They had to do their part of the bargain. In the time of Purim, when the physical aspect of Judaism was threatened, they prayed to God reminding him of the bargain—he should keep his part.

I believe during the Holocaust the covenant was broken. Maybe it will be renewed; perhaps later, maybe it was renewed even then, on a different level. So many Jews kept their faith or even strengthened it. But it was broken, because of the clouds and because of the fire.

HJC: Stars are another symbol in a couple of books, I think.

EW: Yes, especially in *The Beggar*. It's an ironic symbol, too. All these symbols are ironic symbols. When God made his promise to Abraham, he said, "Thy descendants will be compared to the stars and to the dust, not the sea." Stars were a symbol of promise and here again, in our time, stars, like the clouds, became to me all the eyes that are trying to see but cannot.

Harry Golden has suggested that the Jewish people should call their own ecumenical council for the purpose of forgiving Christians their sins against the Jews. This council would take up questions ranging from the Inquisition to quotas at medical schools. In irony, Golden points to a Christian Problem which is sometimes referred to as a "Jewish Problem." As H.A. Overstreet wrote: "It is the mild and gentle people of prejudice who must bear the burden of the moral guilt." It is the mild and gentle people Elie Wiesel is properly obsessed with reaching.

The opposite of love is not hate he observes, but indifference. I remember teaching in a New York City grade school at the time of Adolf Eichmann's trial. Our students had a debate—Resolved: Eichmann should be executed. Participants prepared well and were assisted by other members of the family. One defense tactic was ingenious. The charges, as outlined by the affirmative team, were incorrect. "Six million Jews were not killed. Only four million were." This was a Christian, denominational school. *Indifference!*

Edward Gargan has noted that "the separation which existed between the Jews and their Christian neighbors before the rise of Hitler left the Jews helpless when the murderers came to collect them for the furnaces." Indeed, to whom could the victims turn? The Vatican, for example, remained silent. (Once, when it did protest, the Papal Nuncio hastened to assure officials in Hungary that this act was not "from a false sense of compassion.")

This rejection, the anguish over centuries of persecution, is found in all of Wiesel's writings. In *Night* he tells the story of the death of his father in a camp—of the death of many others too, and of the death of the spirit in him. The "night" of the title symbolized the author's wanderings through spiritual chaos. Wiesel's second book, his first novel, *Dawn*, tells of a Jewish boy who finds faith in a continuing Judaism as he tries to but cannot hate a British officer he must execute in Palestine. This "inability" to hate foreshadowed an incident in Wiesel's own life when he revisited Germany long after the war and lamented his behavior there. As he narrates in "Appointment with Hate," which appears in *Legends of Our Time*: "I answered questions, I shook hands. I even smiled back. And then I could bear no more of this civilized behavior: having lost my taste for hating others, I began to hate myself."

This man who does not even know how to hold a gun has forgotten nothing as his book about the Holocaust, published a quarter-century after the event, *One Generation After*, proves. But he cannot hate, which keeps his vision clear. It is never blurred by propaganda or prejudice. He hasn't the facile answers of the advertiser who convinces us about political parties, ideologies or racial and national attitudes. Rather, Wiesel resubmits the everlasting questions: Who is God? Who am I? What is my relationship to God? What is my relationship to man? All of these questions are implicit in all of his fiction, but some more specifically than others.

The Accident emphasizes, Who am I? A narrator, not certain of the answer, attempts suicide but then is helped to will to live by others who coped better with that question.

The Town Beyond the Wall comes to grips with the discussion of man's relationship to man. So does Weisel's tale of friendship, *The Gates of the Forest*, in which a man faces life after a new friend sacrifices his life for the other. The search continues in *A Beggar In Jerusalem*, while the question of God is joyfully examined in *Souls on Fire*. (The question is there in *Night* also, but the mood is utterly changed.)

In *The Jews of Silence*, Wiesel publishes a reporter's eye-witness view of Soviet Jewry and here again, the basic questions are at least implicit. As objectively (but not without feeling) as he can, Wiesel explains what he saw—particularly that the fear the Russian Jews experienced was far greater than he had imagined and that this fear was absolute. In his commitment to honesty he wonders, is this mass paranoia? But he learns of "the attempts being made to annihilate the Jewish soul by eradicating all memory of its historical identity." He learns also of Jewish informers. He visits Babi Yar where, in a twenty-four hour span, probably 10,000 Jews were murdered and not a Russian Christian protested or even missed a half-hour's work.

But Wiesel also saw the dancing, singing Jews, especially the young, who insisted that he tell the outside world of their celebratory Jewishness. He found that their condition is at once more grievous and more hopeful than he had anticipated.

Wiesel went to Russia to learn why the Jews there had remained silent for so long. He found that they regarded their silence as an oath of fidelity and that they remain true to the pledge regardless of the sacrifice it may require. But the title of the book is intentionally ambiguous. Wiesel writes about the quiet Jews in Russia and to the silent Jews around the world who do not help or protest in any way on behalf of their sisters and brothers. In a tone of prophecy he writes: "That the Jews in the free world do not heed this . . . will never be forgiven them. Of that I am sure. For the second time in a single generation, we are committing the error of silence."

Wiesel's final sentence in the book is this: "But what torments me most is not the Jews of silence I met in Russia, but the silence of the Jews I live among today."

What troubles me is that this appeal is only to Jews. Wiesel seems to have little hope that Christians will be of any assistance.

5 / ה

*S*omewhere in Transylvania, in the shadow of the Carpathians, very near the most capricious frontier of Eastern Europe, there is a dusty little town called Sighet. It is a town like many others, and yet it is not like any other. Quiet, withdrawn, resigned, it seems almost petrified in its own forgetfulness; and in the shame that springs from that forgetfulness. It has denied its past; it is condemned to live outside of time; it breathes only in the memory of those who have left it.

This was my town once; it is not my town now. And yet it has scarcely changed at all since I left it twenty years ago. The low, gray houses are still there. The church and the butcher shop are still facing each other. The synagogue, deserted now, still stands at the corner of the little market square.

It is this fidelity to its own image that makes the town seem strange to me. By looking like itself, it has betrayed itself. It has lost the right to its name and to its destiny. Sighet is not Sighet any more.

For a long time I had had a burning desire to go there. For a week, an hour, a minute—just long enough for a single look. To see it one last time and then to depart, never to see it again.

Nowadays, in spite of the Iron Curtain, distances no longer matter. Anyone at all may leave from anywhere at all and arrive at Sighet, by way of Bucharest, Cluj, and Baia-Mare, by airplane, by train, by car, in less than seventy-two hours. But not I. For me the journey was longer. It was to take me back to where everything began, where the world lost its innocence and God lost his mask. It was from that I started on my journey to Sighet. . . .

"We're coming near," said the driver. Where were we? At the foot of the mountain, thank God. The danger was past, we were in the valley. Sighet: 40 kilometers. Sighet: 30 kilometers. A multitude of huts formed a hedge along the road. Villages sprang up before our headlights and were immediately swallowed again by the night. Far away, there were a few blinking lights. Sighet: 20 kilometers. The car, an old Volga, picked up speed. Sighet: 15 kilometers. "We're coming near," the driver repeated in a heavy voice. His words sounded like a threat. He was taking me to a rendezvous. With whom? With death? With myself? Sighet: 10 kilometers. Sighet: twenty years.

(*Legends of Our Time,* pp. 145-146, 148-149.)

HJC: I notice the parents of the main character in several of your books seem to portray what I am taking to be two poles: reason and faith.

EW: That is because of the autobiographical cut on it. Except for *Night*, my works are not autobiographical—here and there I try to bring in autobiographical data and moods. My father really was reason and my mother was faith. Therefore, the parents are always drawn to different poles.

HJC: Since you mention autobiographical aspects, I want to ask—
it's just personal—but was Maria (in *Gates of the Forest*) a real
person in your family?

EW: No.

HJC: Never had that kind of experience?

EW: No.

HJC: Beautiful character.

EW: The whole *Gates Of The Forest* is fiction; there is nothing in it
which is "true." I brought in Maria in *Gates*, and the Count
too, to show that there were good people, simple people, on the
outside as well. Otherwise, it would have been a total conflict
—on the one hand the Jew who was the victim and on the
other hand, the entire world.

There were Marias who helped here and there. There were
others who helped—and help was possible—so Maria becomes
the example of what all the others could have become.

HJC: Aren't there two instances where the character meets a young
lady in Paris in either a restaurant or bar or someplace? I think
there are two segments. . . .

EW: Yes.

HJC: Is that autobiographical?

EW: No. The other autobiographical items have to do with very
concrete, secondary elements. I did have an accident in New
York.

HJC: You did?

EW: And I was badly injured. I was given up. But I did not attempt
suicide. I used the knowledge that I got for my purpose. There
was no girl. But I wanted to explore suicide and I also liked the
enclosure: what is more of a prison than a cast? Since I had the
knowledge I said to myself, "Why not use it?" I could have told
the story elsewhere with less realism. But the event took place.
I did have an accident in New York which made me stay.

Again, how fate works. If it hadn't been for the accident, I
think I would not have stayed in this country and I would not
have become an American citizen. I was a stateless person and
I came here as a journalist on a stateless document, a French
travel document. I had the accident and for almost a year I was
an invalid. I had to prolong my American visa.

I went to the Immigration Office in a wheelchair and an official told me that I had to extend my travel document which was valid for only one year. (By the way, this is a chapter which I haven't written yet but which should be written one day: I made some allusions in *The Town Beyond The Wall* to the life of stateless persons in our times—the refugees, the stateless, uprooted persons. Unbelievable! Their fears, traumas, humiliations and miseries.)

Anyway, I asked the French Consulate to prolong my document. I was a bona fide United Nations correspondent. The French Consulate said, "No. According to bureaucracy, regulations, you must go back to Paris. If you are a foreigner, you must be in France to extend your papers.

I said, "How can I? I'm in a wheelchair," Nothing doing. I made the trip a few times: Immigration, Consulate, Immigration, Consulate. Finally, the Immigration Officer said to me, "There is only one way of solving the problem. Why don't you become an American citizen?" That reconciled me to the American bureaucracy.

Since then I'm grateful to America. Even when I oppose some of the Administration's policies I do it out of a sense of gratitude toward this country. Nowhere else—with the exception of Israel, of course—did I encounter such a human attitude. That's how I became an American citizen and that's why I stayed here.

HJC: Buy why New York? The place that is so opposed to solitude and silence?

EW: In the beginning I had to stay in New York. I was a journalist accredited to the U.N. My paper paid for my being in New York. That lasted, until, I think, 1966 or so. When I gave up journalism, I had to choose some other means. For very practical reasons I chose New York. Now I don't like New York, I don't like big cities any more. I would like to leave and, as a matter of fact, we were going to leave New York for good had it not been for my commitment to City College which rearranged and changed everything. We were supposed to go away and stay in a small village somewhere, but not a big city. There are too many pressures, too much violence, too many fears and distractions which I don't like.

64

The first builder of cities was Cain. That's how he's referred to in the Bible. After he killed, he began building cities. Not villages, cities. So there is Cain—Cain lives very well in the city. I don't want to.

HJC: So it's the theme of city versus country coming out in your life?

EW: Yes, as I said, I wish I could leave but I cannot.

HJC: You do not write in Hungarian.

EW: In Hungarian, no.

HJC: You made a decision to refuse to do that?

EW: I don't know Hungarian well enough. I knew it when I was young but not well enough.

HJC: It's not your native tongue?

EW: My tongue was Yiddish.

HJC: But Transylvania at that time—Sighet was in Hungary.

EW: No, it was in Rumania. It used to be in Hungary and then, when I was born, it was in Rumania. In 1939 or so it rebecame Hungarian. At home we spoke Hungarian. But I learned first in Rumanian, then Hungarian schools and I didn't know either of the two languages very well. My mother tongue was Yiddish. I studied modern Hebrew before the war.

HJC: So, it isn't a matter of your turning your back on Hungarian?

EW: I did. It was closer to me than French, for instance, or English. Had I wanted to write in Hungarian, I would have had an easier task but I didn't want to; I even tried to forget Hungarian. The Hungarian language reminded me too much of the Hungarian gendarmes and they were brutal. . . . My first breaking point was when I saw what they did to us. We came in contact with their policies earlier than with the Germans and they were nasty, cruel, sadistic. It hurt more than the Germans; we *expected* the Germans to be ruthless, anti-Semitic. Even today when I think of the Hungarians, it's beyond me. Why were they so brutal? There was no reason. So I try to forget Hungarian. I cannot.

It's easier to learn a language than to forget one. I could have written in Hebrew or in Yiddish. Why I chose French, I don't know; maybe because it was harder. I'm sure that symbolically it meant something to me: it meant a new home. The language became a haven, a new beginning, a new possibility, a new world. To start expressing myself in a new language was a defiance. The defiance became even stronger because the French language is Cartesian. Reason is more important than anything else. Clarity. French is such a non-mystical language. What I try to transmit with or in and through that language is mystical experiences. So the challenge is greater.

HJC: When did you learn English?

EW: In India, of all places. I was there in 1952. I didn't know a word of English then. I invented my own method again. I withdrew totally in silence and absorbed the language, just as one absorbs air or sounds. So I learned English in India. Not perfectly, but I could work with it.

HJC: By listening to the spoken English?

EW: Yes, by listening and then by reading. Alone. I never had any teacher in English.

HJC: And you are now a teacher.

EW: Yes, I try to be.

HJC: What are your ideas about the teacher's role in education?

EW: I have heightened respect for teachers now—I mean for true teachers—because I see the importance of what they must accomplish. Until I began teaching, I wrote or spoke to unknown people. Now I see a group regularly and I almost see the results of my teaching. I feel a heightened responsibility and therefore, I take it so seriously.

I invest four hours of preparation for each hour of teaching. In the seminars we study Hasidic or Midrashic Texts, ten lines in two hours. What I try to teach these students is to question texts; to engage in dialogue with them and to question not only those who wrote them but all those who read them before us. When you come to Scripture, for instance, you have many interpretations that you must find when you approach the text. That goes for novels and poems as well.

While you do that you not only give your student a methodology, you give him much more—a certain respect for the text, for people, for questions. I know that the role of a teacher in one's life is primordial. In our tradition, the role of the teacher is so important that if a disciple is exiled by law or by court, the teacher is exiled with him. One has the right to deprive the disciple of liberty but not of study, not of his teacher. The teacher suffers and goes with the disciple into exile. I understand it better now because one can do without many things but not without a teacher.

HJC: Is one of the teacher's roles to transmit—am I saying this right —the notion of the importance of the everlasting question?

EW: Yes. *The* question. And to show the importance of man in the question. The question should not be abstract; it must always have a bearing on reality, on real life, on the real person.

What do we give the student: a key, a code. Today, I believe, the teacher must give more: he must give an example. I cannot go on writing and teaching one way and behaving another. I don't believe anymore, for instance, that today the writer has privileges of not behaving according to certain ethical principles. In the past we forgave the artist and the writer too much. That may have been good a hundred years ago, thirty years ago, but not today. Today I demand from a writer a moral commitment as well, a human commitment. The teacher must be an example.

HJC: And the teacher receives as well as gives?

EW: You know that. You are a teacher. The Talmud says, "More than I have learned from my masters, I have learned from my disciples." That is true. In my case, I learn from contact with my students. Not because they can give now, yet; but I give more to myself than I give to them, simply by being forced to prepare, interrogate and explore. I feel gratitude towards them.

HJC: And part of this being forced to explore is the challenge that students are constantly giving to the teacher?

EW: The challenge, but also their presence. I feel responsible for them and because I do so, I must live up to that responsibility.

HJC: You were born in 1928?

EW: 1928, on Simchat Torah, which is a Jewish holiday—a celebration of the law. September 30th, according to the Gregorian calendar.

HJC: You went to school in Sighet?

EW: Yes. Later on, in high school, I went to Debreczen. I was a kind of external student and once a year I used to go there to take exams. That means I really made an effort only one month a year, the last month of the exams. Otherwise, I spent sometimes ten or twelve hours a day studying Torah. When I say "I", I mean all of us: Jewish children there really studied.

When I see today what children are doing in schools and how they are complaining, then I think about those I knew in Sighet. We used to get up at six in the morning and go to *cheder* or *yeshiva* and study. The studies: Scripture, Talmud and then other, more complicated commentaries. I thought I knew—now I know I didn't—Talmud. Now I recognize that our educational system was not so good. It meant simply repeating after the teacher and remembering by heart a certain number of pages every semester. I knew hundreds of pages. It didn't amount to anything. Only when I came here to New York and discovered a very great teacher, Saul Lieberman, the greatest Talmudist of our time—only when I began studying with him (and I still do)—I realized how much I didn't know of the beauty in the Talmud. So that was really my childhood. My childhood was a normal and abnormal Jewish childhood; ten or eleven months a year filled with study and prayer.

I didn't have much inclination for games. There were four children in our family; I had three sisters (two older, one younger)—I was the only boy. I didn't participate much in any other activities except study. I loved to go to the Rebbe, a Hasidic master in my town or to go to Gross-Vardein. One of my special joys was to go to a village to see my grandfather, Dodie Feig.

I had a grandmother, my father's mother, in Sighet. She was a widow and I'm named for her husband. She was a saintly woman. I speak of her in *The Accident*. She knew, I think she was the only one, with the exception of Moshe the Madman and Mrs. Schecter, who became mad in the train. My grandmother knew that she was going on her last journey because when we all left, underneath her clothes she had on what we call in Hebrew, *tachrichim*, which are the funeral clothes.

HJC: Your grandfather, Dodie Feig; did he live on a farm?

EW: Yes.

HJC: What did he do?

EW: He was a Hasid. Most of the Jews there were farmers. He had, I think, a few acres with cows, horses, goats.

HJC: Would you go there to play?

EW: Not to play. I used to go to listen to his stories and to sing with him. I loved going there! He was a very beautiful man with a white beard and good eyes. Naturally, I remember him because he was *the* Hasid in the family.

HJC: Have you repeated any of his stories in your work?

EW: Oh yes. In *Souls on Fire* I repeated many of his tales. *Souls on Fire* is dedicated to him because of his influence on me. We were very, very close. He lived in a village called Bitskev which was seven kilometres from Sighet. But we didn't have cars; we used to go by horse and carriage. It was really farther away than from here to Paris or from here to Israel. Each trip was a festivity, a holiday.

    In 1944, when the Germans entered, contact was cut between us and him. We lived in different ghettos. I never heard from him again.

HJC: In many cases, the Jews had to be identified, did they not, by non-Jews for the Germans?

EW: Identified in what way?

HJC: As Jews.

EW: They were identified when the Germans came—even before the Germans came. After all, Hungary was an ally of the Axis, so they had anti-Jewish registration and Jews were marked as Jews. There were all kinds of restrictions: in universities, practices and commerce. But when the Germans came, the government behaved even more viciously. Then it really began. The Jews everywhere had to register first and then put on the yellow badge. And then the ghetto. . . .

    Very few even thought of hiding because they didn't know what for. We didn't know what Auschwitz meant. If we had known, even partially; if we had *heard* at least some of the tales, by authoritative people; if the Israeli leaders would have warned us not to go . . . it was 1944 after all. If the Jewish leaders in America had warned us not to go on transports, I'm convinced that many would have escaped. It was possible. We were 15,000 Jews in our ghetto with two Germans and some fifty Hungarian soldiers guarding us and mountains all around us. We could have escaped; the Russians were twenty kilometres away. But we didn't know. No one cared to tell us.

HJC: What were some of the restrictions before the Germans came?

EW: I don't really remember too much. I was too young. The normal things.

HJC: Travel and so on?

EW: Travel and citizenship—we were second rate citizens, period. That means there were numerous restrictions in universities, there was fear in high schools and then beatings. Anyone had the right to do so. No one was punished for beating Jews. In 1941 or 1942, many Jews were declared stateless and deported to Galicia where they were all killed. Only Moshe the Beadle returned. And lost his mind. . . .

I don't remember too much; I didn't even suffer too much. I was too absorbed in my own studies. I was more aware about what went on three thousand years ago than what was going on in the present. I could have described to you the events surrounding the lives of Abraham, Isaac and Jacob and David but not what was going on in Budapest, in the government. I couldn't have cared less.

HJC: Do you have any actual memories of Christians, or at least non-Jews, who did something heroic or that you encountered personally . . . worthy people?

EW: I must begin my answer by telling you that my father used to be a kind of intercessor with the authorities in Sighet. Whatever happened in the community, they came immediately to him (and if I have now such a sense of community, maybe I inherited it from him). If anyone was in jail, immediately my father was alerted; if anyone was sick, it was my father who raised funds for doctors; if anyone had troubles, he came to my father. Even today many people write to me saying they are alive thanks to my father's efforts.

He saved Polish Jews in 1941 or 1942, when they escaped somehow to Hungary. He managed to save them in a strange way. He discovered a regulation that if a Jew or any person is caught with foreign currency, he must immediately be sent to Budapest. Usually, when Polish Jews escaped to our town (it was very near the border) and were caught, they were shipped back to Poland to be massacred. The only thing to do was to keep them as long as possible. My father got hold of currency (dollars and pounds) and smuggled it into the prison. Thus, hundreds of Jews were shipped to Budapest. They were saved —in jail, but saved.

My father always had good connections with the authorities: he bribed them. He had a good acquaintance, a Hungarian police chief, or chief detective, whom he would bribe. He would give him money and gifts; I don't even know what kind of gifts. When the Germans came and began persecuting us and decided to put us in a ghetto, the detective told my father: "You may go into the ghetto. Don't worry. If something serious should really be about to happen, I will find a way to let you know."

Then came the ghetto. We spent a couple of weeks there.

Then came the Saturday afternoon when the Germans announced the first deportation.

Our house was on a street corner. One side of the house faced the ghetto; the other side faced another street which was not part of the ghetto. We had to nail these windows shut with wooden plates so we couldn't see outside the ghetto. In one room lived the Reich family, our relatives whom we had taken in. (The Reich daughters are now in New York.)

That night, while we were waiting for my father to come back (he was trying to find out from the police what was happening) we heard someone knock at the window outside but we were afraid to open it. A couple of minutes later, there was another knock. When we opened the window, there was no one there. We believed then that it was that detective who came to warn us. Maybe, had we opened the windows. . . . Yes, that detective was a good man.

I remember in Auschwitz the first speech by the Polish chief of the block, Block 17, I even mention it in *Night*. We were new; we didn't know where we were. He told us. And he said we must remain human and try to show solidarity towards one another. . . . These words of humanity and kindness in *that* universe . . . well, he was unique and he was good; he was special.

Then, again, in Buchenwald. The chief of our block was a Czech. We were then in a children's block and we were all destined to be shipped out of the camp in its last days. All the Jews were summoned to be deported and killed. He somehow changed the registration. He managed to save this entire block —a few hundred children. These people stand out.

HJC: This is not much testimony to non-Jews.

71

EW: Not much. Even these two were prisoners. I cannot forget when I remember the looks on the faces of our neighbors at home when we left. No shock and no sadness, no pain.

HJC: The indifference of the man in the window?

EW: . . . the window . . . the indifference. . . . It's not an uplifting picture that haunts us when we look back.

Many years after the war, people ask, "Why didn't you escape? Why didn't you run? Why didn't you rebel?" Well, in our case, we didn't know. But even in Poland. . . . the question is so unfair. Where could *they* have run? They were as much in danger by the Poles as by the Germans. There were, I heard, some Christians who behaved. Very, very few.

When the Israeli authorities began assembling material about what we call "the just Gentiles," those who saved Jews during the war—each was to get a medal of recognition because we are a people of gratitude—I don't think they found a thousand.

HJC: Do people contact you from all over the world?

EW: Oh yes. I receive hundreds of letters monthly.

HJC: Mostly all Jews?

EW: No; sixty percent Jewish. My readers seem to be about sixty percent Jews, forty percent non-Jews. But all are religiously concerned. Someone who is irreligious, who has no interest or no passion for anything religious or spiritual, apparently doesn't read my books.

HJC: So, you're not getting any crank letters?

EW: Oh, I do receive crank letters. But innocent crank letters. People who are mad because they feel I have a special sympathy for madmen. So, I do get a lot of "mad mail" too.

HJC: Do you get letters from people saying, "Why don't you let the subject die; we have other problems?"

EW: Not letters, no. But I had a few encounters like that. Questions, mainly. Reporters when they interview me . . . once I had it from a priest, of all people, in Canada who said, "You know, it's enough after all." Some Israelis say, "It's enough now. The past is the past. Let's normalize our relations with Germany; it's not the same Germany any more." Some so-called "friends", in quotations, believe it would be better for me not to be into that subject anymore. They suggest it would be better not to live with those ghosts. Others simply say, "Well, we would like you to write about other things now."

But then, I do receive other letters, letters of encouragement saying, "At least *we* understand." Mainly they come from young people which is always very moving. Sixteen year old boys and girls. Very moving.

HJC: Did your mother work on the farm when she was a young girl?

EW: I don't think so, no. My mother was a highly cultivated person. She was one of the few who finished high school. In our place, Jewish girls didn't go to high school. And to be the daughter of a Hasid in a high school. . . ! A fervent admirer of German literature—she used to quote Goethe and Schiller by heart. No, she did not really work on the farm. But then, she was a strange mixture of an educated person and a Hasid, with the fervor of a Hasid, a firm believer in the Rebbe and, at the same time, open to secularism.

Her dream was to make me into a doctor of philosophy; I should be both a Ph.D and a rabbi.

She was famous in her Hasidic milieu as the daughter of my grandfather, Dodie Feig, and also because she was quite a person in her own right.

Usually, when a Hasid comes to a Rebbe he presents his request, 'though he doesn't write it himself. He gives it to the scribe who in that way makes *his* livelihood. The scribe writes the request for different reasons: one, to make some money; two, many Jews didn't know how to write in those villages; three, the Rebbe had to be accustomed to one handwriting. My mother was among the very few people who refused to use a scribe; she paid him the money (so he would not be deprived of his livelihood) but she wrote her requests herself.

I remember a terrifying episode with my mother and her Rebbe. I have here in New York some distant cousins. One of them is still profoundly religious, still a Hasid, a fish handler. I have another, even more distant cousin, a doctor. One day I received a 'phone call from the doctor saying, "You must come to the hospital right away because our cousin is sick. He needs immediate surgery and he doesn't want to have it unless you come." I jumped into a taxi and rushed to the hospital.

My cousin was lying there, waiting for surgery. He said, "I don't want to undergo surgery unless you give me your blessing first." So, I said, jokingly, "Really, you know, you are now so religious, even more than before. Your prayer will be heard sooner than mine; you deserve to say prayers more than I." He said, "Nothing doing! If you don't give me your blessing I refuse to go into surgery." The doctor warned me: "Every minute counts."

I hesitated. I felt undeserving. But finally, I had no choice. It was either/or. So, I gave him a blessing. I heard enough blessings in my life; I knew what words to use. He went into surgery and it lasted a couple of hours. Eventually, he recovered. Not because of my blessing but because my other cousin was a good doctor.

Several days later I brought up the subject again: "Now tell me the truth. Why did you ask for my blessing? You know that I am not what I used to be!" "Well," he said, "Your blessing *is* important." "Why?" I asked. He said, "Do you remember the last time the Rebbe was in Sighet?" "Yes," I said, "I do." I was very young then, age eight. I went to see him, as usual, with my mother.

But it was a special visit. I came inside his room and he teased me. He asked me questions; I answered. Suddenly, he said to my mother, "Please leave us alone." She went outside and I remained with him. He took me on his knees and again we talked; I don't remember about what—we talked probably about my studies, Scripture, Rashi, Talmud. We talked and we talked and I looked at his beautiful illuminating face; he was a beautiful being and this was reflected in his eyes, his voice.

After a half-hour or so he let me go and said, "Send me your mother." My mother went in; I remained outside. Hundreds of Hasidim were waiting. When she came out she was crying bitterly. I was afraid I might have said something to insult the Rebbe, misbehave; who knows what I did? I asked her, "Why do you cry?" She refused to say. I went on nudging her for weeks on end: "Why did you cry?" for she went on crying. She did not tell me. Eventually I forgot and I didn't insist anymore.

So, I said to my cousin, "Yes, I remember the last time because my mother was crying." Then I told him the story and he said, "Well, I was there. As a first cousin of your mother we were close; I know why she cried." When he said that, a shiver went through me. I realized that there is no accident in life; there are only encounters. He had to become sick and I had to be in New York just to find the answer to that question.

I said, "You *know* why?" "She confided in me that day. When she went in, the Rebbe told her, 'Sarah, daughter of David'—that's how he called her—'I want you to know that one day your son will grow up to be a great man in Israel but neither you nor I will be alive to see it. So, I want you to know now.' That's why she cried and cried."

And my cousin said, "Well, if the Rebbe said that about you, I think that your blessing does carry weight."

HJC: And your father; what did he do?

EW: He was a merchant. He had a grocery store. He sold everything. A grocery store in our town meant everything. He worked hard from early morning to late at night. He was more absent from home than present because either he was in the store or he was working for the community.

I remember him, mainly, when he was jailed. He was jailed after one of those people whom he helped escape to Budapest, revealed his name under torture; he was arrested. For two months or so he was in jail. I know now that he was tortured there but he never spoke of it.

When I see him, I see him on weekdays either running to do something or in the store, working together with my mother and sisters, working to the point of exhaustion.

I remember him on Saturday, at home. Then he studied— he was a Maskil, an emancipated Jew. He didn't have a beard but he was religious. What Jew wasn't religious then? He was the one who forced me to study modern Hebrew. Thanks to him, many years later, when I needed a job I could immediately become a journalist for a Hebrew newspaper although I had never been in Israel for any length of time. He said to me, "Listen, if you want to study Talmud, if you want to study Kabbalah, whatever you want to study is all right with me and I'll help you. But you must give me one a hour a day for modern study." And I did.

He brought me books of psychology; I read Freud in Hungarian. He brought me books about astronomy. He made me discover the modern Hebrew literature. He adored music, just as my mother did, but especially cantorial music.

I really discovered him only later, in the camps, because I was closer to him then than before. Before, he had the entire community on his mind; then, the entire universe was reduced to him and to me.

HJC: How did he meet your mother, do you know?

EW: I heard it later on from a Hasid of Wizhnitz, one of the people who helped my father save Jews. He's in New York. He told me that one day, my grandfather and his youngest daughter came into Sighet from the village where they lived—Bitskev. My father, who stood in the street, saw her in the coach and he was stunned by her beauty. He ran after her, which is unusual in our place; he ran after her to find out who she was. He found out from the coachman, not from her. He went back to the village, spoke to my grandfather and won her.

HJC: Beautiful. It *is* unusual.

EW: It is. In those times, in those places. . . .

HJC: When you left the camp, after the war, you went to Paris?

EW: Yes. Not straight to Paris, however. I was among four hundred children in Buchenwald who did not want to go back to our places of origin. We were asked where we wanted to go. I didn't know. I wanted to go to Palestine; we all wanted to go to Palestine but the British wouldn't give us certificates. From that point on we were ready to go anywhere.

HJC: These four hundred were from that block that was saved?

EW: Yes. I think they asked me, "Do you want to go to Belgium?" Why not? Belgium, Belgium. To me it was all the same. I didn't know countries; I didn't know geography.

I think while we were travelling to Belgium with some American officers who escorted us, DeGaulle heard about us and he had the train rerouted to France. We were taken over

76

by a Jewish organization called O.S.E. and we were led to a place called Ecovis, in Normandy, to a castle. There we were supposed to recuperate.

The war was still on; it was the end of April. We were liberated on April 11; I was sick for ten days at the end of April.

Then, in Ecovis we were divided. First of all, there were a hundred who were religious and three hundred who were not. We hundred kept together. I didn't know a word of French. One day I wanted to get some books, religious books, to study Talmud again.

I went to see the director. His name was Mr. Wolff, I think. While I was there, he was talking on the telephone. I heard him mention my name but since he spoke in French I didn't know what he said and I was too shy to interfere. When he finished his conversation he said, "Your sister just called from Paris."

I said, "It's impossible! My sister, how can she. . . ? First of all, I don't think I have a sister. Before we left Buchenwald there were all kinds of lists that were brought in by the American army and other organizations and I checked all the lists to be sure that none of my family remained. My father died, with me. I was sure that my mother and my little sister . . . but I had hoped that my older sisters survived. I checked the lists. I didn't find their names. That's why I didn't go back to Sighet. Otherwise I would have gone back. It's impossible! If one of my sisters survived, what is she doing in France, not in Sighet? Even if she is in France, how does she know I am here?"

He tried to call back but the person who had called, did so from a post office. "But she gave me a message," said Mr. Wolff. "You should take the train tomorrow; she will wait for you in Paris."

In those days the trains didn't run that often. For twenty-four hours I really didn't know what to expect. I came to Paris and there she was, my oldest sister, Hilda. And then I learned something extraordinary.

She was together with my other sister, the middle sister, Beatrice; they were together in the same camps and they were sure that I didn't survive. Hilda, after the liberation, had met a

French inmate, a French Jew from Algiers, and they decided to get married. She came with him to Paris while Beatrice went back to Sighet.

One day Hilda opened a newspaper and saw pictures; one of the pictures was of me. I didn't know that *journalists* had come to interview us. I didn't know why they had spoken to me. I didn't know why they had taken my picture. I didn't even know what "journalist" meant; I had never seen a journalist in my life—I had never read newspapers. Had it not been for that picture, I think it would have taken many years for us to meet.

In fact, Beatrice, who went back to Sighet to look for me, heard that I died because I was so sickly at home. I was always weak and frequently went to see doctors. I suffered from headaches and all kinds of illnesses. What I didn't know was that if I was so weak it was because I didn't eat. Mondays and Thursdays I would fast. I was leading my own ascetic life and my parents didn't know. They simply saw I was losing weight so they dragged me to all the doctors. If anyone was to die in the camps it would have had to be me. Beatrice was in Sighet, waiting several weeks. Maybe someone would come back? Some people came back bringing the news: I did not survive.

I think it took another year before contact was re-established between the three of us. One sister is in France; her son is in Israel—he just had a boy, too. My other sister* is in Canada and she has two children (a boy and a girl) and her boy, who also has my father's name, just became a Bar Mitzvah.

HJC: So, you stayed in Paris?

EW: No. I didn't stay with my sister; she didn't have the means to support me. I stayed one day with her and went back to Ecovis.

They divided the religious and the non-religious and we, the religious, went to another place in France, Ambloy. There I began my studies. Later, we went to Paris, to Taverny. That's when I met the mysterious Jew, Shushani, of whom I speak in *One Generation After* and in *Legends Of Our Time*—the one who became my master.

*She died of cancer shortly after this conversation took place.

—E.W.

Some of my former friends are now Rabbis in Brooklyn. I went on studying French—mainly French to absorb the language—and I entered the Sorbonne to study literature, psychology, philosophy, psychiatry—in a very autodidactic manner. All I wanted was to study.

Later I went to India, having in mind to write a dissertation on comparative asceticism: Jewish, Christian and Hindu. I had written a huge volume, some six hundred pages or so, which I'm afraid to open—I'm sure it's not good. One day I will and probably will have to rewrite it. I didn't complete my studies. I had to work as a journalist and it was hard work.

HJC: In France?

EW: In France.

HJC: For a Hebrew newspaper?

EW: Yes. I had to be at its disposal. They sent me around too much.

HJC: Is that the newspaper that assigned you to New York?

EW: Yes. The *Yediot Ahronoth;* it's published in Tel Aviv. But I was its correspondent in Paris, then in New York.

HJC: You covered the United Nations, I believe.

EW: Then I covered the U.N., yes.

HJC: Then had the accident?

EW: Then I had the accident.

HJC: You met your wife here?

EW: Yes. Through friends.

HJC: Is she from here?

EW: No, she was born in Vienna and after the Anschluss her family moved to Belgium; when the Germans entered Belgium, they moved to France. They were in a concentration camp in France; then they escaped to Switzerland. They went back to Belgium for a very short time and she came here in 1950 or so.

HJC: You were already publishing?

EW: Yes.

HJC: And had she read your works?

EW: She read me. Her French is perfect. So is her English. Therefore, she is the ideal translator.

HJC: What do you do for a change of pace?

EW: I work; I don't know anything else. I never relax. When I'm tired, I listen to music. But I always work; I cannot not work. I haven't had a vacation, I think, since before the war.

HJC: What is work to you?

EW: Justification. I have to justify every second of my life.

Lazarene literature, that product of confinement, is increasingly being recognized as an important genre of writing. It is truly the literature of resurrection from the living death. Contemporarily, it is the political prisoners who are occupying the role of literary Lazaruses; we need only to cite Alexander Solzhenitsyn's *One Day In The Life of Ivan Denisovich* to exemplify the point. East Germany's Horst Bienek, in *The Cell*, is another qualifier. So are the brothers Berrigan, Daniel with his poems and letters (and his introduction to Bienek's novel), and Philip with *Prison Journals of a Priest Revolutionary*. There is Arthur Koestler too, and the late Turkish poet Nazim Hikmet, as well as the untranslated work of the Costa Rican novelist, Jose Leon Sanchez. France, especially, seems to have contributed a special kind of concentration camp literature: for example, Robert Antelme describes the horror of experience in *L'Espece Humaine*. David Rousset portrays a real world which is indeed separated from a real world in *L'Universe Concentraitionnaire* and Jean Cayrol attempted to develop a new Christian world concept in a concentration camp existence. Dostoyevski, St. John of the Cross, Oscar Wilde and St. Paul come to mind more naturally, perhaps. With *Night*, Elie Wiesel takes his place with the best of these writers. This book is a supreme representation of a whole sub-genre of literature which can be labeled under the heading of Holocaust Literature. *The Diary of Anne Frank* belongs there as do Chaim Kaplan's *Scroll of Agony*, Victor Frankl's *Man's Search For Meaning, The Night of the Mist* by Eugene Heimler and a sadly glorious list of others.

It would not be an excess to read Wiesel in mythological terms—his non-fiction as well as his fiction, with the author as central character. Perhaps we can best understand him as the hero as Joseph Campbell conceives that figure: the person who retreats from the world (secondary effects) to the psyche (causal zone) and through his experience illuminates—to clarify—the real difficulties. He then returns, transfigured, to the outer world to teach the rest of us the lessons he has learned. Wiesel's actual physical retreat from the world took place at Auschwitz; his spiritual retreat continues daily. However, his insights he shares with us periodically in his writings and his lectures. The significance of these, and of Wiesel's own lifestyle, are not to be underestimated. What Arnold Toynbee says about the continual rebirth of ongoing civilization may be applied on a personal level to Wiesel. Each new work of his, while in a sense solving a particular problem, creates tensions toward a new one. This is the mark of health according to Toynbee, who maintains that for a civilization to merely achieve a solution (and to simply see that resolution as the goal in itself) is for a civilization to begin to atrophy.

Night, in fact, the keystone of the mosaic which Wiesel is constructing, has "caused" many tensions for him. In it, he met the problem of his father's death courageously, a question which is never far from his mind. Not only does the absurdity of that event trouble Wiesel, his immediate reaction to it pains him. Just for an instant young Eliezer felt relief of a burden when his father was taken away. A natural reaction yet an unacceptable one for the boy whose childhood was not allowed him. In *Dawn*, he examines contemporary history, a question he can treat differently in *A Beggar in Jerusalem*. Of course, other questions are presented in each of these books besides the ones suggested here. The point is that the very solution of one creates a tension and therefore other questions to be resolved. The corpus is not atrophying.

Wiesel understands the double paradox that Campbell's mythological hero represented. First, the hero is nothing if he is not a part of his community. It nourishes him and helps to determine him. But at the same time he must separate himself from that community in order to transcend its limitations and become that group's leader. The second part of the double paradox has to do with mysticism which is, by definition, a meeting ground of opposites: the divine and the earthly. The double paradox is "effected" in the hero's plunging to the omphalos of the universe, the navel, the very core of existence, which each of us carries in himself, and then willingly returning to the secular community to share his new knowledge.

It is not enough, Campbell teaches, for the mythical hero to separate himself from his sisters and brothers. Acceptance of the call is a mere beginning. He must travel the roads of trials and frustrations, danger and pain, as he seeks to learn precisely who he is. Even when he has been granted the boon of self knowledge, his work is not nearly done. The hero must be willing to return to us who, consciously or not, await his teaching. Once the hero comes face to face with Truth, it may be considered a simple thing for him to wish to remain in that situation—possibly a kind of euphoria. But Odysseus refused to remain the eternal lover of the goddess, just as the true social hero will return with his Truth to his people.

Today, a person like Wiesel, unique in any age, is possibly more unique than ever. Contemporarily, we are in danger of being a truly absurd world. Russian Literature has the tradition of the superfluous man. I submit that Solzhenitsyn has expanded that to include a superfluous society. The trend may be in the direction of a superfluous universe. Today's saints or mythological heroes all seem to carry national banners. Campbell has pointed out that we are capable of supporting only local symbols, we cannot "manufacture" world symbols. The modern hero must rediscover and make apparent world symbols, Campbell teaches. If for our purposes we could distill Toynbee's teachings, I believe they would reflect a similar message. Elie Wiesel is one such hero.

6 / ו

W hen the great Rabbi Israel Baal Shem-Tov saw misfortune threatening the Jews it was his custom to go into a certain part of the forest to meditate. There he would light a fire, say a special prayer, and the miracle would be accomplished and the misfortune averted.

Later, when his disciple, the celebrated Magid of Mezeritch, had occasion, for the same reason, to intercede with heaven, he would go to the same place in the forest and say: "Master of the Universe, listen! I do not know how to light the fire, but I am still able to say the prayer." And again the miracle would be accomplished.

Still later, Rabbi Moshe-Leib of Sassov, in order to save his people once more, would go into the forest and say: "I do not know how to light the fire, I do not know the prayer, but I

*know the place and this must be sufficient." It was sufficient
and the miracle was accomplished.*

*Then it fell to Rabbi Israel of Rizhin to overcome misfor-
tune. Sitting in his armchair, his head in his hands, he spoke
to God: "I am unable to light the fire and I do not know the
prayer; I cannot even find the place in the forest. All I can do is
to tell the story, and this must be sufficient." And it was sufficient.*

God made man because he loves stories.

(*The Gates of the Forest*, Introduction.)

HJC: What does it mean to you to be a writer?

EW: Essentially, it means to give testimony, to bear witness. Witness
has two different connotations. In the Christian tradition a witness is often a martyr. In the Jewish tradition a witness is a kind
of messenger. The witness says, "That is how things are."
"Amen," in Hebrew means, "That's how it is." The witnesses
that we are make us into messengers.

The story I tell is always the same. Whether I write about
the Talmud, Hasidism or contemporary events, my function is
still the same: to transmit what I have received and then to try
to understand it; to communicate visions that other people
cannot have or cannot express, either because they have not
had them or because they were too afraid to acknowledge, understand, or receive them.

To be a writer also means to correct injustices. The injustice in history is that some things are forgotten but others
remain. People are dead but others survive who do not remember the dead. When entire communities are swallowed up
and nothing remains, then it's an injustice. All this makes me
into a writer but the word "writer" really does not apply. I see
myself much more as a storyteller. The things that I have to
say I have not said yet and perhaps they will never be said.

HJC: Yet, these things somehow might be apprehended by your
readers without having been said?

EW: Yes. We can call it a "secret." There is a secret in every work of art; there is a secret in every tale—a secret which only the teller knows and sometimes the reader receives without knowing it. To give you an illustration: a good translator is one who translates not only the words and the music but also the secret of the book although he is unaware of that secret. There is a secret in every tale, book and novel and that is what makes the unity of the work.

HJC: Then the writer who prostitutes words is committing an artistic sin?

EW: He's committing a sin, period! Words are no longer innocent; words are dangerous. We have learned that in our time. But then, we have learned that in all times. . . .

    The first sin is a sin against language. I think man begins to sin by prostituting language. The writer who does this prostitutes himself and therefore, his characters, his subject, his obsessions, his past which—if it is his past—then it is blasphemy.

HJC: What is a story?

EW: The story that *I* try to tell is, first of all, a story of night which the *Kaballah* calls *shvirat hakelim*—the breaking of the vessels —that something happened at the origin of creation, a cosmic cataclysm.

    Our story is of the same nature. Something happened a generation ago, to the world, to man. Something happened to God. Certainly something happened to the relations between man and God, man and man, man and himself. Rather than explore the story in abstract terms, I try to tell the real story. But this story we tell by not telling.

    In all of my books, I think, I indicate the impossibility of communicating a story. By indicating that impossibility, I already hint at a certain story, a certain aspect, a certain level of a story. The story itself, I'm afraid, will never be told because maybe only God can tell it—to himself, not even to man. The magnitude of the catastrophe, the absurdity of the tragedy, the silence of the world, the responsibility of the accomplices, the very fact that it could have happened, and the very fact that it could have been avoided—all these elements make it into a mystery, almost a religious mystery, with theological implications. This is really the story that we try to tell.

The story is built as a foundation, when night descended upon mankind, when night invaded man's conscience. Once it is said—done—we have to build another universe on it or go under. So, all the other stories result from that story.

Night, my first narrative, was an autobiographical story, a kind of testimony of one witness speaking of his own life, his own death. All kinds of options were available: suicide, madness, killing, political action, hate, friendship. I note all of these options: faith, rejection of faith, blasphemy, atheism, denial, rejection of man, despair and in each book I explore one aspect. In *Dawn* I explore the political action; in *The Accident*, suicide; in *The Town Beyond the Wall*, madness; in *The Gates Of The Forest*, faith and friendship; in *A Beggar In Jerusalem*, history, the return. All the stories are one story except that I build them in concentric circles. The center is the same and is in *Night*. What happened during that Night I'm afraid will not be revealed.

HJC: There are other people telling other stories, some not so momentous. Is there something that you can say about simply the abstract notion of "story"? Why are we so anxious to hear stories and why are people so bound to tell stories?

EW: I can only speak about true listeners and true writers. True writers want to tell the story simply because they believe they can do something with it—their lives are not fruitless and are not spent in vain. True listeners want to listen to stories to enrich their own lives and to understand them. What is happening to me happens to you. Both the listener and the reader are participants in the same story and both *make* it the story it is. I speak only of true writers and true readers and true listeners. As for the others, they are entertainers and their work doesn't really matter. I don't want to go into names but there are very few great storytellers and great writers today.

Actually, I believe that today literature has changed its purpose and its dimension. Once upon a time it was possible to write *l'art pour l'art*, art for art's sake. People were looking only for beauty. Now we know that beauty without an ethical dimension cannot exist. We have seen what they did with culture in Germany during the war; what they called culture did not have any ethical purpose or motivation. I believe in the ethical thrust, in the ethical function, in the human adventure in science or in culture or in writing.

Our generation has special privileges but special obligations. I believe that every writer today, no matter who, Jewish or not Jewish—but particularly Jewish—must write with the Holocaust as background, as criteria. Once he takes this as a background, as a yardstick, he will be careful in writing. He will not prostitute his words; his responsibilities are such that they are paralyzing. When one writes, thinking of those invisible victims who should be his readers and are actually his writers (because he's writing their story), then one is very humble and very daring at the same time—in writing a sentence or when translating an image.

Today, to write about any other thing seems frivolous, unnecessary. I often lose patience when I read a novel of two, three, four hundred pages about the same love story—he loves her, she doesn't love him. All this has been said again and again, better or worse; it doesn't matter. The fact is that it's almost irrelevant when you think of what happened or the stories that we can tell. A fragment of a spark of the fire that we have seen is more important than all the other books together.

HJC: When did you first realize that you would be a teller of tales?

EW: I knew I was going to write even before the war but I didn't know what I was going to write. I come from a Hasidic milieu, from a religious background. I didn't read novels before the war, only religious books. At the age of twelve or thirteen I even wrote a book: a commentary on the Bible. (I found some of the pages after the war when I went back to my home town.) Had it not been for the war I would have written, probably, another commentary on the Bible or on the Talmud.

After the war I absorbed. I absorbed not only the suffering, which was not mine alone—suffering everywhere in the camps —but I absorbed, unwittingly, perhaps unconsciously, the obsession to tell the tale, to bear witness that every single person shared and nourished and had to put forward. I knew that anyone who remained alive had to become a storyteller, a messenger, had to speak up.

But I was afraid, afraid not to live up to the task. I was afraid of saying the wrong things, of saying too much or too little - or becoming sentimental, or romantic, or too literary. I waited ten years. I did make a vow in 1945 to wait ten years. I remember when and how I decided to become a teller of tales.

After the liberation I became sick and it's strange how it happened. I hinted at it in *Night* but it's not the full story. April 11, 1945, when the Americans came, we were some 20,000 left in Buchenwald, out of 60,000 or 80,000 and we hadn't had food for a week or so. Suddenly the Americans came and brought their food but they didn't really know what they were doing; they gave fats. 5,000 people died immediately from blood poisoning. I remember they gave me a piece of ham. Had it been during the war I would have had ham, although I'm a religious Jew and I don't usually eat ham. During the war I would have been pleased to eat it. But it was already an hour or two after the liberation so I was a free man. When I put that ham to my lips my body rebelled; I lost consciousness immediately and I was sick for ten days or so—unconscious, in a coma —blood poisoning or something. My spirit didn't know yet that I was free but my body knew.

I remember when I got up I was very weak. One day as I was looking in a mirror, I didn't recognize myself. That was the first time I saw myself in the mirror since I left home. I then decided that since everything changes—even the face in the mirror changes—someone must speak about that change. Someone must speak about the former face and that someone is I. I shall not speak about all the other things but I should speak, at least, about *that* face and *that* mirror and *that* change. That's when I knew I was going to write.

HJC: Did you know when you wrote *Night* how you'd go about using that as the basis for the stories?

EW: No. It could have remained my one and only book. My other stories were not autobiographical. I wrote *Night* first in Yiddish in 1955, I felt because I was brought up in that language, I owed something to it as I owe much to my childhood, the language of my childhood and to the people who spoke Yiddish, to the culture which vanished. It was published in Argentina. Then I translated it; I shortened it and condensed it in French.

Meanwhile, I met Mauriac and we had many conversations. I couldn't find a publisher for that book in France or for that matter in America; Mauriac took the manuscript and he brought it personally to one of his publishers. That was the beginning of my adventure in literature.

But when I wrote it in 1955, while I wrote it, it might have been the only book I would have written. To me it would have been enough. I did what I had to do. I think, in re-reading it, I suddenly realized that to stay with the past was not enough. We must take the past and transcend it.

I began thinking of the other books as well, maybe because *Night*, in the beginning, had some eight hundred pages and I cut it down to a hundred and sixty. Suddenly I was left with six hundred pages and I thought, "Well, there are enough pages here for other books." But I decided to destroy them, not to be tempted. Then I said, "Since I had six hundred pages about *Night*, I must have in me other pages about other things, other times," And I went on writing.

HJC: During this ten year period did you make notes or were you thinking about this.

EW: I never spoke about it; I never made notes; I only read. I read every single book that appeared on the Holocaust. I still do. I'm a voracious reader of Holocaust Literature and World War II Literature. I still want to understand what happened. And yet, I went on doing other things. I studied. I learned French first, studied French literature, went to the Sorbonne.

In 1948, when Israel was born and Palestine was divided, I wanted to go to Israel, I went as a volunteer to the recruiting station and the doctor looked at me, gave me a checkup and offered me his visiting card saying, "Come to my office. I have to treat you; you are not strong enough to go." I was unhappy. I wanted to see Jerusalem; I wanted to be there although I was never a political member of a Zionist organization. To me it was a messianic event with which I wanted to be associated.

I became a journalist and as such I went to Israel at the end of 1948 or the beginning of 1949 for a couple of weeks. I came back to Paris, went on studying but remained a journalist, attached to an Israeli newspaper, travelling all over the world. I felt the urge to know the world. As a journalist it was easy to travel, not because we had money—the paper was a poor paper and I was even poorer then. But in those days, with a press card, you got free trips on ships, on planes. I explored the world and went to North Africa, Africa, South America, India and elsewhere. That was a period of ten years—taking in, studying, learning, meeting people and finding my own area of possibilities and their range. I explored the dimension of silence in me. There were weeks and weeks and weeks when I didn't speak, not a word, voluntarily—not one single word. I wanted to see what one does with silence. I even studied psychiatry. For two years I was a student in a psychiatric institution, Ste. Anne. So, these were ten years of preparation and reflection.

HJC: Reporting is a different kind of writing. Was that helpful to you?

EW: It was helpful and destructive at the same time. Journalism differs from literature. It helped me with discipline. I had to file daily stories. I had to write everywhere: on a plane, on a train, in a cafe or the cable office. At the same time it was destructive because the events were boring and repetitious. There are very few new things that happen in our world.

I could have written, I think, throughout the year, ten cables but always the same cable, either about Dulles or about Acheson; sometimes a war in Indochina was being discussed in the U.N., sometimes another war in Africa. Someone made a survey and found that the *Daily News* never used more than 800 words, *The New York Times* maybe 2,000 words. Poor and unexciting, it can be destructive. Fortunately, I was never politically minded and I don't understand much about politics. I don't know how I managed to file political cables without betraying my ignorance. Oh, I know how, really: I copied *The New York Times*—we all did. We took from the city edition and we simply quoted from the *Times*.

I liked human stories much better. There I *did* work. But then, the deadline was not so pressing and I had time to write. Basically, it's not the same writing. A writer should give up journalism the moment he can. I had to stay with it for practical reasons; that was my means of survival, to go on living.

HJC: And, as you mentioned to me before, not a very handsome means.

EW: It wasn't much, no. I didn't make much.

HJC: To Frank Reynolds, you said that you tried to create meaning in a universe without meaning. Is that quite literal?

EW: I think so, yes. I think this is what we are all trying to do, not only myself. We all try. Every writer today attempts to achieve the same thing. We live in a generation of darkness, so much darkness that we want to bring some light to it or, at least, to give an intensity to the darkness. There is so much suffering that we try, at least, to evaluate it and see where it comes from, if not to redeem it.

There is so much absurdity in this world that we try to fight it. The enemy is indifference. We attempt to fight that enemy. And, yes, when you think about it, all of our experiences were without meaning. The Holocaust was an absurdity and, therefore, we can say an ontological phenomenon. It had no meaning. Even from the German point of view it had no meaning. When they gave priority to trains with Jews, carrying Jews to the camps, priority over military trains carrying troops to the front—it was madness! Sheer madness! Even from their point of view it had no meaning.

HJC: How do you feel when you finish a book?

EW: When I finish a book I feel physically exhausted. But I never finish it because I always smuggle into every book one sentence which is the substance of the next book—a Jewish tradition. When we finish reading the Torah on Simchat Torah, we must begin again the same Torah at the same session. Because we never finish, we never begin . . . it's a continuous process. Thus, when I finish a book I have already begun another. Naturally the anguish comes: whether I have not said too much— it's never too little but too much.

I write every book three times, three versions. The first one is usually very long and after I have finished it, I wait a couple of weeks and then I write another version of the same book without referring to the first one. The third version, actually, is a combination of the two but it's already a cutting down, a condensation. When the book is finished, I have only one fear: maybe I haven't cut enough? Nothing but the substance must be said, nothing but the essential. We have no more time, no more patience to play around with words. The feeling is really of anguish.

The reward comes later. When I meet certain people I see that my ambitions were fulfilled. I want to change certain people. I want to change their destiny, at least for one second, to alter their views of destiny, to give them something, to make them vibrate. When it happens, it's a rewarding feeling.

Even more rewarding are the moments when I meet survivors. They come from everywhere and they say, "You know, you say what we cannot say. You speak for us." Then it's most fulfilling because I feel that I have really done what I should have done. More rewarding than that: if, when I meet the children of those survivors and they come to me (I have them now in my class) and they say, "We cannot speak to our parents because our parents don't talk or talk poorly or they are too shy. Because of you, we understand our parents." Then I feel reconciled to my work.

HJC: It seems impossible that you could work with an editor.

EW: I don't work with an editor. When I give a book to a publisher they don't change a word. To work with an editor is only an American institution. This is not so in Europe. There a writer must give the full book to the publisher. If he's not capable of doing that, he's not a writer—at least that was so in my time. Now it may be changed. America has influenced Europe, not the other way around. Here, when my book comes to the American publisher, it's already a finished product, simply to be translated.

HJC: What about translators?

EW: I used to work with some translators. Now I work with one— my wife. She's doing very well; she doesn't really need my aid. She's an excellent translator.

HJC: For what you are doing, it would seem that it would have to be somebody who is that close to you to do the translating. But what happens when you get into other languages?

EW: Oh, I don't know. I'm always afraid. I'm afraid to read. Years ago, when I got the first draft of some translations, I was flabbergasted. The inadequacy, the misunderstandings, the poverty. I'm afraid to see some of my translations. I have Japanese books here and, fortunately, I don't know what they are saying. But then, maybe some are good. Norwegian, Dutch, some are good I'm sure. But I am afraid.

HJC: You understand what Solzhenitsyn is going through in that respect?

EW: Oh yes, certainly. I understand him in more than one way. To be a captive writer and to try to write against the whole regime, fight it with words, is not easy. We try to fight the whole world with words. The difference between Solzhenitsyn and our kind of writing is that he writes *with* words, therefore, he writes these huge books in the Tolstoyan tradition. We write *against* words. We don't trust words as much any more. At the same time we trust them too much; we know their power. Therefore, we write so little, so condensed; we are unsure of ourselves. We are afraid of words betraying us and us betraying the words. Solzhenitsyn doesn't have that fear and he can afford to write these huge, huge novels.

HJC: How about your feeling when you begin a novel? We talked about when you finished a novel.

EW: It's the beginning that counts. If the first page reads well, if I hear it well, then the novel is there. If not, then I don't continue. I wait until I have the first page in me and then the words begin to sing and I hear the melody. The novel comes and there's no more problem. It's the first page that determines the novel although I don't know what will come later. The first page is really the dominant one.

HJC: You say you don't know what will come later. In that sense, do your novels "write themselves?"

EW: Yes, the first draft certainly. As with every other writer, I'm surprised by my own discoveries. I don't know what I'm going to do with my characters; I don't know what situations I'm going to choose or be involved in. I don't even know what names they will take.

I only know the first page and the melody. If the melody is there, what we call in Hasidism the *nigun*, the chant, is there then it works. If not, I don't begin the novel and I go to the other side of my work, the non-fiction, the research and Talmud, Bible, Hasidism and I wait until the melody will come.

HJC: But you do devote a regular period of time a day. . . ?

EW: Yes. I write four hours every day. It's very often not good; I throw away many pages but I write for those four hours. Again, it's the discipline. I don't want to waste a day. From my childhood I had this obsession that to waste time is a sin. One of the greatest sins is to waste time because it is given by God and to waste our time is to waste his.

I don't understand people who claim to be bored or who want to "kill time." To "kill time" is another expression which is so typical of our generation, of this society. To "kill" time? We should *save* time. I don't remember who said it, I think Kazantzakis did—"If I could I would take a box and go to all the places of entertainment and say, 'Please give me a few moments of your life.' "

HJC: Yes, Kazantzakis.

EW: I need time. I never have enough. In order to be sure that I will not waste a day, I devote at least those fours every day to writing. But as I say, it's very often not good and I simply throw it in the basket.

HJC: But what is cut away is still not totally lost?

EW: It's never lost because in a book the pages that you cut remain. Somehow you feel, the reader feels the density of a page if there are in that page many others which were cut out. First they have to be there. But the true reader feels that here were pages which were cut out.

HJC: I don't want to read anything into this, but is the beginning a rather painful kind of experience?

EW: No. After I finish writing then comes the pain and anguish. While I write I do so with a sense of celebration. I write to celebrate something. I write only when . . . again, I'm too Jewish for that: I believe in fervor, in exultation and I write in a state of exultation. If not, I don't write. There is no pain except the very special pain of exultation. Exultation without pain would not be genuine.

More pain comes later. When the book is finished and before I send it away to the publisher, then I start thinking:

"Maybe I said too much; maybe I've done injustice to one of these characters?" Only at this moment do I feel pain. More pain comes afterward, when the book is published, when you get compliments for things that you didn't deserve—wrong compliments—or when you get criticism, negative criticism, again about things that you didn't deserve. But the undeserved compliments are more painful.

HJC: Have critics been helpful to you, some critics in some ways?

EW: No. I'm much too arrogant in my own eyes. I don't think that anyone in the world could know better than I what to say about the things that *I* have to say. Furthermore, I know, and I am honest enough, I think, to admit it to myself—if anyone else could have written any one of my books, I wouldn't have written it.

I don't read all the critics; I only read a few in the beginning or the criticism of my friends. I want to know whether *they* understand me. Otherwise I don't read. I'm afraid to be hurt and I'm too sensitive so I don't read too many. As to my own writing, I really cannot tell you that I changed one line or one word or one direction of a book because of any critic—or because of any editor. That wouldn't be acceptable.

HJC: Writing is a form of prayer, is it not?

EW: I think I quoted Kafka who said, "Writing is a form of prayer." What is a prayer? It's a kind of selection of words against others, of the exclusion of some words before others. In doing this, you create a certain zone of piety, a certain zone of expectation, of waiting and of silence which surrounds the prayer and the prayer comes out of itself. This is a prayer to God about God.

Basically there is such a need for worship in all of us today that I write for that purpose—to adore, to express that sentiment, that need, that quest for adoration. Whom can we worship today? Whom could we follow? Whom could we admire today as I could when I was a child? I pray and I try to transmit that prayer but that does not necessarily mean religious prayer. I think secular people are wrong when they believe that praying involves religion. They need prayers more than we do. Strangely enough, there is today a return among the scientists to religiosity. They know more than we that they have reached a limit and that now it's time to go back and see what was at the beginning, what the beginning meant.

HJC: Prayer is a discipline also.

EW: Yes it is. But a true prayer can be against discipline. Prayer of ecstasy is a prayer against discipline. Celebration is against discipline.

I would say prayer envelopes every form of creation but prayer must be linked to creation. Man cannot pray if he is alone. Through his prayer he is not alone. Man trusts in the universe, totally in solitude, in isolation, without any link to anything. Why pray? Only if man is part of a society, part of the universe, and part of God does prayer have a meaning. Then prayer can become song.

In Hasidism prayers are of a rich variety. There can be intellectual prayers, long prayers, short prayers, simple prayers. The most famous example is of the shepherd, in the story of Baal Shem, who one Yom Kippur was in the synagogue. While all the other people prayed and prayed, he at one point took out his whistle. All the congregants were angry with him except the Rebbe who said, "His prayer was heard. He meant it." If one wants to pray, one doesn't need words or a set of prayers. One can do it with a whistle if one means it.

In the Old Testament we read that man is created in the image and likeness of God. In my judgment what the writer of Genesis means for us is that we reflect God most truly by participating in his creation. We are daily called to renew the face of the earth, renew ourselves and environs, to continually create and recreate. This means as parents (responsibility for as opposed to simply the propagation of children—Gabriel Marcel points out that full parenthood does not mean generation; all animals can do that much), as teachers, neighbors, carpenters, drivers—all aspects of life including writing, painting, sculpting, singing, composing and all of the so-labeled "fine arts." What is said, below, then is said of the writer (and of a particular author here) but can be modified to include potentially all humans in their various activities.

Writers are ministers of the word if they are serious in their approach. This is a self-ordained priesthood to which they belong, one freely chosen with all of the obligations therein implied. In this context, I suggest that if you could break off a piece of the Holy, it would be in the form of a Word. But, of course, advertising for products and for candidates, as well as ideas—including wars—has as one of its goals subversion of the word. Is God "great?" So is a particular automobile. Do we have obligations to ourselves in life? One of these, we are told, is to drink a certain beer regularly. Is health a problem? It is not; we simply have to use the right pills to ease the pain.

One result of all of this has been an increase in the use of obscenities in written works. At least there is nothing ambiguous about the four letter word. When a pope or a president gives an address, people may argue for years about what he meant. Had he used obscenities, they might have understood more clearly. But there is a better way and Wiesel has chosen it. This way includes having a reverence for the word and an understanding of its potential sacredness, as well as its potential sacrilegiousness. Wiesel fears telling only the partial truth, let alone telling a lie. Here's what he says in *A Beggar in Jerusalem*: "In the beginning there was the word; the word is the tale of man and man is the tale of God." In a previous novel he had written that, "The meeting of the place and word is a rare accomplishment on the scale of humanity."

He speaks of the creative word in the tradition that the American Indian does, the Indian whose medicine men did not cure with their herbs but with their incantations. The word has a magic, a quality of mystery to do this. Through its repetition an Indian might become well, or brave, or successful in the hunt or in love. The genesis story of the Uitoto begins this way: "In the beginning the word gave origin to the Father." For Eskimos, the hunt is participated in by both men and women; the men do the physical assaulting, the women chant to the gods for success. The failure of either party to carry out the task properly results in the failure to catch.

What this all leads to is that life and art must not be compartmentalized. Wiesel would agree with Solzhenitsyn, who wrote of "Art—For Man's Sake." In *Legends Of Our Time*, Weisel writes that, "Some writings could sometimes, in moments of grace, attain the quality of deeds." In a later book, *Souls On Fire*, he is even more precise: "Some words *are* deeds." So Wiesel can understand the advice given to a Hemingway character who wants to write a particular story but cannot begin. He is told to write one sentence that is true. Presumably another true one will follow, and so on.

Understood in all this is the risk the author (creator) takes in stripping himself to give us the truth. What he does, he understands, will have to be inadequate. We may, if we wish, laugh at his nakedness. He must have what Alfred Adler called, "the courage of imperfection." This courage exists in an artist's willingness to make a mistake as he searches for truth, comprehending that from his mistakes he and others can learn more truth. Or, as Rollo May explains in an early work, *The Springs Of Creative Living*, "The healthy, creative human being is he who admits his imperfections frankly, without the shame that makes for deceit, and remains at the same time continually responsive to the commands that emanate from perfection in God."

Wiesel understands all of this very well. In *Legends*, he writes this paragraph (part of which I italicize for emphasis):

> "Souls dead and forgotten return to earth to beg their share of grace, of eternity; they need the living to lift them out of nothingness. One gesture would suffice, one tear, one single spark. *For each being participates in the mystery of creation; each man*

*possesses, at least once in his life, the absolute
power of the* Tzadik, *the irrevocable privilege of the
just to restore equilibrium, to repair the fault, to act
upon the absent.* Condemned to go beyond himself
continually, man succeeds without being aware of it
and does not understand until afterward."

This paragraph is followed by a simple sentence which
summarizes Wiesel the creative man:

"And now let me tell you a story."

7 / ז

*O*n his way to the mass grave,
the historian Simon Dubnow
exhorts the Jews of Riga, his
companions in misfortune: "Open your eyes and ears, re-
member every detail, every name, every sigh! The color of the
clouds, the hissing of the wind in the trees, the executioner's
every gesture; the one who survives must forget nothing!"

In Birkenau, a member of the Sonderkommando in charge
of maintaining the furnaces, compiles, by the light of the
flames, reports and detailed statistics for future generations.

Everywhere, at the very core of distress and death, young
militants and wizened old men make notes, consign to paper
events, anecdotes, impressions. Some are only children: David
Rubinstein and Anne Frank.

Behind the walls of the Warsaw Ghetto, Emmanuel Rin-

gelblum and his hundred scribes have but a single thought: to gather and bury as many documents as possible—so much suffering, so many trials must not be lost to History. Since European Jewry is doomed, it becomes imperative to at least preserve the scorched vestiges of its passing.

Poems, litanies, plays: to write them, Jews went without sleep, bartered their food for pencils and paper. They gambled with their fate. They risked their lives. No matter. They went on fitting together words and symbols. An instant before perishing in Auschwitz, in Bialystok, in Buna, dying men described their agony. In Buchenwald, I attended several "literary" evenings and listened to anonymous poets reciting verses I was too young to understand. They did not write them for me, for us, but for others, those on the outside and those yet unborn.

There was then a veritable passion to testify for the future, against death and oblivion, a passion conveyed by every possible means of expression.

(*One Generation After*, pp. 38-39.)

HJC: While I fully expect them to be a part of this record, these are the questions, the answers to which particularly interest me and one of the reasons why I'm grateful to be here. I'll start with the last question first so that you can see where I am going. I too want to find out who I am. How can I do this?

EW: Formerly I believed that one must be totally alone to find oneself. I still believe so but I believe that even this loneliness, this solitude must be within the human condition: to be alone but faced with another person being alone. Then you can find out. If you face someone, your child or your wife or your friend, then you can find out who you are; but the *other one* is essential, indispensible.

Still, I believe solitude is important, as are silence, honesty, madness. Madness may be the ultimate outcome. The person who faces himself alone is like someone closed in a cell with endless mirrors and the endless reflections may drive him mad—the eye of the eye of the eye of the eye. *The other* can become a menace or a rescue.

HJC: Does the other have to be as aware of this search?

EW: No. The other has to be aware only if the other, too, wants to find out who the other is.

HJC: But a child, for example, couldn't. . . ?

EW: Not that a child couldn't know, but a child could become the other. A child wouldn't do it for himself but for the other. In our tradition a child always suggests the presence of God. God appears to us not only as innocent but as vulnerable as a child. And when we say the other we mean the other as God too.

Ultimately, what does God want from us? Why did he bother? This is a question that can never be answered. It hasn't been answered in any religion. What for? I understand *our* purpose—for him.

Once a Hasidic rabbi came to see me in class. He wanted me to do something which I don't like to do—organize a group of men of the arts and letters for his Rebbe at the Kennedy Center in Washington.

I said, "How can I do this kind of thing and how can I go there and speak? I wouldn't be able to utter a word. It's not to my taste, not in my character."

He tried to convince me. He said, "Well, do you think that the Rebbe does what *he* wants to do? Do you think that the Rebbe wouldn't be more pleased to study and not to be involved in practical affairs?" Then he went further and he said, "Do you think that God likes to be here, part of our society, to see what is being done in his name and on his behalf? Do you think *he* doesn't suffer?"

I didn't want, of course, to offend him but the answer was, who asked him? I say with all reverence. I say it in fear, not in jest. What for?

There is in the Talmud, I think, only one instance when a poll was taken among the sages: Is it more comfortable for man to have been born or not to have been born? They took a poll and it showed: No, it would have been much more preferable for man not to have been created at all but since he *was* created, he should study and observe the law.

This is a question that hasn't been answered. On our level,

all right, but on God's level. . . ? So what do we do? Rather than say, "Why do *you,* meaning God, bother with us?" we say, "Why do you, man, bother with him or with me, with another man?" Here the *other* is important, simply to give our quest another dimension, a greater one, and sometimes the possibility of an answer to, who am I? The question is not a question limited to myself.

HJC: This leads me to my first question. The broader aspect of this question is something about the meaning of history. What is history? What is history to me, to you, to man?

EW: There are many definitions of history. I always go back to Hebrew. It's a philosophical language; it's the only language that has meaning everywhere.

The letter "A", for instance, is an *aleph. Aleph* means the letter "A"; it means a number, one; a verb, it also means "to tame." "B" is *bet,* the letter "B"; a number, two and the meaning is "house." When you tame the verb you can make it into a house. Gimel, which is "G", number three, means "to reward." Once you go with this system, you have your own reward in the world.

History, in the original Hebrew, has two words. One is *tol-dot,* which means the origins, the births, the series of words and the second is *korot,* meaning events. So, I would say history means a summation of events, rooted in their origins. What it means to me, of course, is more than events; it's the origins to which events link us. As for contemporary history, it is sometimes a mirror and sometimes a glass in the window. Most of the time I feel it as a closed zone where we all belong together and we cannot break out. I cannot break out alone but only if I bring others with me. It's like a boat, to use a parable of Rabbi Nachman of Bratzlav: the fool thinks that because he bought passage on the boat he can dig a hole in it. It's under *his* seat. I cannot destroy my part of history without destroying history as such.

HJC: Both Kazantzakis and Teilhard, as I read them, are saying that the individual is a culmination of all the past and the beginning of all the future. The implications are there again of the great responsibility not only to interpret the past but to be the stepping-stone for the future.

EW: It's a very Jewish concept. We have it in our tradition that the first man, Adam, will also be the last man—he'll be the Messiah. We are living links between them. All of us are both Adam and the Messiah. We contain both. Each time someone commits a sin, he removes the Messiah farther away from Adam. Each time he is good, be brings Adam closer to the Messiah. Before Adam died, we are told, he was shown all the generations. Not only because God wanted him to see what would happen, but also because he wanted to create a link between each generation and Adam. So, we all go back to the origin. All the events must take us back to the source.

HJC: So Adam has seen us?

EW: Adam has seen us. Yes. That means we have been in his eye; we have been in his mind. It also means that we are his link to the Messiah.

HJC: There seems to be an attempt, at least on the part of some, to do away with the past.

EW: They try, but the past always comes back and slaps our faces. I think there is now a reversion. The young people disliked the past until recently. Whatever was the past was not good: they wanted new paths; they wanted new things; they wanted revolutionary things. What was the past was discarded; they thought the past was ugly. Now I think the future to be so desperate and so bleak that even the young people today who are revolutionaries want to go back to the past. They find not only a meaning *for* the present but sometimes an explanation *of* the present.

HJC: "Questions are more important than answers." You have said that several times.

EW: Yes, because the questions remain; the answers change. Again, let's go back to the past. We are still repeating the questions that Adam asked when he was alive. The basic questions are always the same: What am I doing here? What is the purpose of my life? The purpose of my meeting people? What is the aim, God, death, freedom? All the real questions stay basically the same. The answers change and are being revised. They go and come back and go and come back, to infinity.

    What divides people is not the question, it is the answer. If it hadn't been for answers, there would have been no wars.

Question, I think, comes from the word "quest." If people were to share their quest and make it a common quest, there could be a better time, a better fate, a better society. But they, for some reason, want to give answers, maybe because we need answers. The answers are all temporary, while those who give the answers see them as eternal. Hence divisions, dissensions, wars, death.

If I use these ideas so often, it's because I relate them to our generation and to our experience. Those experiences of which I try to speak have no answers, should have no answers. I'm afraid of anyone who comes with a theory, a system, based on that experience. I am suspicious; I don't want theories. I believe the experience was above and beyond theories and systems and philosophies. What remains is the question: How, What and Why. . . ?

HJC: Let's consider man as Job—particularly modern man as Job— or is it only particularly because I'm living now?

EW: That is our way of accentuating our own relationship to the past. Whatever we say about Job could have been said anytime about Job, by him or by his friends. It is because we come after Job and his friends that it has special emphasis. I don't believe history repeats itself because the next time a similar event occurs it is something more. I don't think that because an event has happened already the next time it's going to be easier. On the contrary, whatever comes afterwards is no longer the same. Because we say about Job or to Job or of Job, *now*, certain words, certain ideas, certain concepts, although they might have been already said and uttered by other people, they do take on a special meaning for us. Man today is more like Job than our predecessors. But they could have used the same expressions.

HJC: How should I read Scripture?

EW: I'll tell you how *I* try to read Scripture. I try to read Scripture as living history. I try to bring back Abraham and Isaac and Jacob and Job and Joseph and see them in the light of contemporary experiences. I would like to see Abraham as my neighbor, if not as my father, Isaac as my brother or my son.

I give lectures once a year at the "Y" and usually I begin with a Biblical lecture and I do exactly this. I began with

Adam and went to Cain and Abel, Abraham, Isaac, Jacob, Joseph and so forth. These will be collected in a book soon. What I did with *Souls On Fire* will be done with the Biblical characters. I try to bring them to life. If the story of Abraham and Isaac was limited only to their ordeal, we wouldn't have remembered it. But Abraham is alive; Isaac is alive. We have no mythology in Judaism, only history, only memory. So I *must* be able to see Abraham, Isaac, Jacob and I *must* be able to see Joseph.

For instance, when I think of Abraham, I think of a father and a son during the Holocaust. Who is Isaac but the first survivor? When I see Jacob, I try to understand him. To me, he's the son of a survivor which explains all of his problems, adventures and dreams. When I see Cain and Abel, I see the first anarchists, the first nihilists, who may be idealists—Cain may have been an idealist: he wanted not only to kill Abel, but he wanted to kill Creation and destroy it once and for all because he wanted to repair the injustice done to his parents who suffered for nothing. Joseph—believe it or not, I see him as a forerunner for Kissinger. He was the first Kissinger in Jewish history; the one who left his family at home, went to a foreign country and became the advisor to kings. So, this is how I read scripture, as a fascinating tale; it's a compelling adventure which has a bearing on my life today, and yours, and everybody's.

HJC: As in scripture, so today there are few just men in this world?

EW: Very few. Maybe there are none. If there are, do we know them? Could they live here? No, the world, I'm afraid, is almost doomed, doomed by the past. It will take only the Messiah to save it, to correct history again, to give us back a certain hope. I sound pessimistic; I *am*. There was much evil unleashed then. For nothing. And there was such indifference then.

It still goes on. As I said before, I don't see why any day a madman could not destroy the planet. He could; he'd be mad enough to. Thirty-six just men, in our tradition, or ten, as in scripture could save the world. How could they survive? How could just men survive in Sodom? If Abraham was looking for these ten men in Sodom and didn't find them, it is because they couldn't survive in Sodom. They couldn't coexist with Sodom.

Yet we try to give some room for just men to be just for one second. Maybe that is the answer. One should not try to be just all of his life—it is impossible—but for at least one moment a day, one day a week, one week a year. Not to the entire world but to a few people. You know, when I was young I tried; I was convinced that I would bring the Messiah, save mankind, the entire world. Now I'm much more modest. I try to help one person here, one person there—not even then for the entire world, for the entire life—but for one moment a day for one day.

HJC: The use that you make of time in your novels, or the way you portray time, is as if time were eternally present.

EW: That is the literary form that I chose. I try to link the past to the present. The present and the past are the same to me and I move sometimes seemingly with illogic from past-present, present-past. But I do it, one: because in our tradition and in Hebrew past and future can be interchanged—it's almost the same word. Two: I do it because the time of a novel is not the real time and yet it is the substance of a lifetime. We live seventy years or fifty years or forty years, yet we really live only a few hours or a few days. We collect a few meaningful hours and these form our lives.

In the book I only take the substance. This is the real time. So what I do always happens within a ratio of time: twenty-four hours, usually one night. Most of my time periods last one night in all of my novels. And most take place in a closed location. It's either in the camp (*Night*), or in a cellar (*Dawn*), in a hospital room (*The Accident*), in a cell (*The Town Beyond The Wall*), in a cave (*The Gates Of the Forest*), or near to the wall (*A Beggar In Jerusalem*).

HJC: Andre Schwarz-Bart does something similar in *The Last of the Just*.

EW: Yes. He also takes time and condenses it.

HJC: In his later work he has abandoned his initial theme.

EW: Yes and no. I think he will come back to it. I hope so. *The Last Of The Just* was such a great work of art that he felt he had said everything. But I feel and I hope that he will come back.

HJC: Your telescoping of time, if you will; there's a parallel in your use of space, also, from here to there and from first person to third person.

EW: The problem of identity is always *the* problem which preoccupies every writer and every person. I do it all the time and it's very hard to fully perceive how I move. *Night* was only "I"; *The Accident*, also "I." In *The Town Beyond the Wall* I moved to the third person. Still, most of the people that I interrogated afterwards were convinced it is in the first person while it is totally in the third person with some excerpts in the middle. *The Gates Of The Forest*, too, is from the third person point of view.

Now, in *The Oath*, I have moved in that direction much more. The change between "I" and "he" is frequent and sudden and interwoven; I think I'm pushing the experiment to the last limit, at least for that novel. Actually, that is clear because, who am I?—it is *the* problem. I'm convinced that when the first man, when Adam, opened his eyes and he saw God, he didn't say, "Who are you?" He said, "Who am I?" The question of all questions is not, "Who are you?" It is, "Who am I?" Who is the "I" in me? The "I" that speaks? The "I" that is spoken to? This dialogue, this quest of the real "I," which can never be solved, I try to transmit in my novels as well—in the *form* of my novels at least.

HJC: Somewhere you wrote that he who says "I" says "I" for all men.

EW: Yes. At the core of our being there is only one "I" and when we reach that "I" it is *the* "I", *the* man. When I say "I", I speak for all men who say "I". Ultimately we are two: I and God, I and I. Who is the other "I"? It's when I speak and I say "I", I address myself to the other "I" but then I speak *for* him as well.

HJC: So there is even then a step beyond: we know about I—It, and I —You, and I—Thou.

EW: And now I say I—I. I always try to go one step further. Otherwise I would repeat and why should I repeat? It has been said already. Again, if things that I have to say have been said, I wouldn't say them. If someone else could tell the tales, I wouldn't tell them.

HJC: I see the interchangeability in your novels of father and God and friend. Is this an accurate reading?

EW: Yes. But then there is also the friend, the madman. You should add one: friend and the madman and then the "other." The father is always God, yes. Friend is not always God. We know that God is a father, we know God is a master. But is God a friend? The madman is asking the question and that's why he is mad. Who is mad? Someone who tries to see God. Because then either he dies—according to the Bible he must die; he who sees God dies—or if he doesn't die, he must go mad and maybe he goes mad in order not to die.

HJC: But I also mean specifically the identification of *your* father with God. In a sense when he died, God also died.

EW: What I say there is that when my father died, I died. That means that one "I" in me died. The only time when I spoke about the absence of God, the God who kills, and therefore can kill himself, was when I saw the hanging of one child and two men—a child whom I didn't know, men whom I never knew. Only then did I speak in these terms or at least think in these terms. But not when my father . . . it would have been too easy and I didn't want it to be easy. When my father died, I died. At least, something in me died.

HJC: Is there some way of saying that your books are in a sense a liturgy to your father?

EW: That my books are a liturgy? Yes, all of them. I would like them to be a liturgy: chants, prayers, all of them. But not only to my father. Some to my father, others to all the others: *The Beggar* is to my mother, *Souls On Fire* to my grandfather, *Legends* to my father. I think one day I'll write to my little sister. Always to some member of my family, to some friend I have known. *The Oath* is a liturgy to Moshe the Madman.

HJC: I really want to ask, in relation to some of the questions I've just asked, what does having a son mean to you?

EW: For the moment, it's hard to tell. It's a simple question with a complex answer. In the beginning, surprise. But because of the intricacies, having a son has other connotations as well because he has the name of my father. I discover gestures of my father in him and, in a way, he's my son and my father. Through him, my father will come to life again or at least his name will come back as we have said.

HJC: In the particular way that you have lost a father and now become a father: what does this mean to you?

EW: I think it means supreme defiance and supreme faith against faith. I'm convinced that if I had not been Jewish I would not have accepted the awesome responsibilities of bringing life into this world. It is really the Jew in me that says that we must go on, we must build endurance, no matter what. We must show that although there is no hope, we must invent hope. Although the world is not worthy to have its own children, we must bring these children, hoping that we should change the world.

We must not forget that during the war, in the ghettos, they were still having weddings, children, circumcisions. They had romances, courtships, celebrations in the ghettos. Maybe because they felt that they had to live fast because the time of the ghetto was not the same as time on the outside. Also, I believe they did do to stress their faith, that we cannot be discouraged. We went on having children, even then, because one moment before one dies, one can deny death. And one can create his own immortality.

So I have a son. I feel awe, humility, hope when I see my son. I watch him sometimes for hours on end, simply thinking —in the beginning with tremendous compassion—"Why? What for? I've seen these kinds of children." And yet, I think it's good—it's the only thing to do. Naturally, I may say to myself, "I will try now, because of him I shall try even harder to change destiny, to change the world, to make it better." It's not true. I would have tried anyway, for other children as well. Except in this case it's more concentrated. It has to do much more, I believe, with my father, with my family. He's the last to carry our name. My two sisters had two sons, but they changed their names while my son will carry our name. And names should not be destroyed.

111

HJC: Are you saying here that your fatherhood now is an intensifying of your response?

EW: No. I said I would have done the same thing as before—except here, it's a more concentrated effort and also a more urgent one. What used to be abstract is now concrete: we *must* fight evil, we *must* fight cruelty, we must fight wars, we must fight injustices simply because there is one more life now in the world and this one more life . . . at least I know I'll have to shape it.

HJC: We were talking about the notion of creativity and the values of the word. In *The Town Beyond the Wall* you write that, "The journey to say a word is the meeting of the place and word on the scale of humanity." And in *The Gates of the Forest* you talk about, "In the single word you can understand the mystery of creation." Then, finally, in *Legends*, a different kind of question, I think, comes out of this where you conclude one legend by saying, "No use retracing my footsteps, looking for a trace of the orphan all the way back to the house of my first teacher. I already know the alphabet." These insights are all related, aren't they?

EW: All the three quotations have to do with my obsession with language and silence: to see how one can reconcile both language and silence. When we write, we write with words and these words come from somewhere. These words have already been said and uttered thousands and millions of times. And then there is some mystery that takes place when I take these words and make them mine.

What happens then? I give them my charge; I give them my past; I give them my life. To these words, I give a certain electrical current to make them vibrate, to make them sing, to make them dance. How *not* to use certain words, this is what I try to learn much more than how to use others because the word is a creative act; before you say it, it wasn't there—even those words that were said before you, they are waiting for you to enter life. Once you say them, you make them your own; they become a prolongation, an extension of your own self, of your own creative urge. You take words and you put them into the universe simply by inserting them in one's conscience. There is a certain fear resulting from approaching the word. This is the first quote.

The second quote indicates an attempt to retrace man's quest to the original man, to God. God created the world through the word. In the beginning was the word. He could have done it with thought. Why did he choose words? Words become the link with creation. Any person, when he tries to create with words, is made in God's image. That is a warning: do not abuse words. As my teacher said to me, "With words you can create either angels or demons. Be careful. Do not create demons. Create only angels; create only the good and the humane."

As for the third quotation, this is already related to something else. In *Souls On Fire*, the first legend is about the alphabet. I described that simply. By knowing the alphabet you can reinvent the universe. You can bring the Messiah if you know how to use the alphabet, without even making the words. Once you know the alphabet and you *don't* bring the Messiah, once you know the words and you *don't* redeem man then you waste them. This last sentence in that story in *Legends* to which you refer is a kind of negative self-depreciating comment. Here I am; I know the alphabet and yet, what am I doing with it?

HJC: Scripture tells us that man is made in the image and likeness of God. One of the conclusions that I have personally drawn from that is that at least one of the ways we reflect God is by participating in the Creation. Is this not the sense of what you've just said?

EW: Absolutely. Rebbe Menahem-Mendl of Kotzk said, "In Scripture it is said that God created the world to be made." I don't know exactly the English expression; in Hebrew it is *asher barah Elohim la'asot* ("Which God in creating had made."). And the question is asked in our sources: "Why the repetition?" If he *created*, why "make"? Because God created for man to do, so man could complete. We cannot create; we are too weak to create. But we can recreate: we can complete; we can achieve what he began. I agree, the likeness being that we are partners in creation. That is the great gift, the awesome gift, that God made man, that he elevated him to the rank of partner and when I say awesome, I refer to the legend that I wrote for *The Town Beyond The Wall*, the last legend about man and God changing places.

HJC: So, it requires a response?

EW: It does require a response, yes. One cannot simply withdraw from creation and be human. A man who says, "I am alone, outside the community," is not a human being. Although he is alone, his solitude too is a real solitude, but we don't believe in it. We just hear our solitude.

HJC: As you have told me, "response" is the root of "responsibility."

EW: Yes.

HJC: In your interview with Frank Reynolds, you mentioned something that he did not pick up that I wish, perhaps, you could elaborate on. You said that before, imagination preceded literature, now it's the opposite. Do you remember that?

EW: No. I can't, but I adhere to that idea. Once upon a time, the writer imagined things that were not here. He imagined one's own death, for instance. What are the obsessions in literature: death, childhood, solitude, anger, madness. Once upon a time, we had to invent all these concepts, give them life and then they emerged. Every writer was a prophet in a way because he already anticipated what would happen to him, to his characters, to man or to his readers.

Today, it's just the opposite. Whatever we can imagine has already taken place. Could we imagine, *now*, going to the moon? We are going to the moon. Could we imagine situations in politics: Nixon going to China? Could we imagine China and Russia becoming enemies? Now they are enemies.

The same occurs in every single area of human endeavor. Whatever takes place today is beyond our imagination. This is rooted in our own experience during the Holocaust; the unimaginable became true and therefore became imaginable later. Even today we cannot imagine the past. Even today it's hard for us to grasp, with our fantasy, with our imagination, that the past really took place there. So, rather than imagine the future, we try to imagine the past. Again, the terms of reference are those of the Holocaust.

HJC: Do you read much fiction?

EW: I read fiction but there is not much to read today, unfortunately. I reread now. I think I'm reaching the age—probably you have reached it too—when we reread and we are afraid of rereading because we are often disappointed. Books that I used to think thirty years ago, when I was very young, were great works, now, upon rereading, seem pale, lifeless, bloodless, terrible.

I'll give you an example. I went to Russia. Usually I travel with a lot of books in my suitcase; I have more books in my suitcase than clothes. Why? I'm always afraid, suddenly, I might be stuck without books somewhere, that all the books may be burned. How can I go on living without books? I take books everywhere. In Russia I read a lot travelling. Suddenly, I had read them all and was without books and I panicked. In Leningrad I entered a bookstore, wanting to buy French or English books. The only French books they sold were Communist books. Or the only novels I could find were Romain Rolland's. So, I decided I would reread *Jean Christophe* which, when I was young, made a terrific impact on me. I was disappointed. Is this the man whom I admired in my youth? Terrible. The book is over-written, overstated.

I read new novels too. I try to read them but I am afraid to read bad books. I mean it. I believe just as good books make you wiser, bad books make you more stupid. There's a danger in reading bad books. I developed a method of opening a book and going through a few pages and then a few more, further inside, to know whether it's good or not. I am sure I am unfair because they too are a part of literature. Stupidity too is part of man and part of our condition. But, I feel an urgency in life, in my life—I don't have time. I'm afraid to lose time, to waste time. So I only read good books and there are not too many that I reread.

HJC: Am I right, you don't want to discuss what the good books are?

EW: I would not mention names.

HJC: I thought, maybe, we'd just better stay away from that.

EW: Good. Why should I hurt other writers? I cannot hurt people.

8 / ח

Messrs. Karl Ragnar Gierow, Anders Ryberg,
Anders Osterling, Johannes Edfelt,
Artur Lundkvist, Lars Gyllensten
The Nobel Committee of the Swedish Academy
Borshuset 111 29
Stockholm, Sweden

Gentlemen:

It is with great pleasure that I respond to your invitation
to nominate a candidate for the Nobel Prize for Literature.
The choice for me is a very easy one: Elie Wiesel.

In this post-Holocaust era, which may well be a pre-
holocaust period as well, man must look into himself to

find the faith and the hope which will not only sustain him but which will require him to sanctify rather than destroy the world in which he lives. That Elie Wiesel's writings could embody this hope, in spite of his personal history as a youth, including Auschwitz and Buchenwald, is remarkable. That he could do so with the simplicity and stylistic excellence he has achieved is a tribute to both his art and his ability to universalize the meaning of his experiences. Wiesel is able to do this because he has found out who he is.

And who is he? He is a Jew.

He is Job, of course. But he is also one of the Last of the Just—a man 4,000 years old who has absorbed the spirit of a People and transmits it through his very existence. But he is non-Jew, too, because he is Man and speaks for all of us and to all of us. May I presume to review with you his twelve books, whose eloquence I will only be able to approximate, which make up the mosaic of his *ouevre*.

Night, Wiesel's first book, is the autobiographical account of his loss of faith in the concentration camps. It is the story of a fifteen year old boy who is shipped to an outpost of death in a freight train, separated from his mother and sister forever, doomed to watch his father perishing daily. In spite of physical and psychological torture, this boy endured. He proves, as Francois Mauriac has written, "one of God's elect." It is clear from Wiesel's later works that Mauriac's judgment stands.

It is with *Night* that Wiesel develops his "statement by understatement" technique. No sentimentality, no exaggeration, the style is to render a vision simply, without embellishment. Who could embellish on the theme of the Holocaust? Hence, when mother and father, daughter and son get off the train at Birkenau, the reception center for Auschwitz, and an SS officer orders "Men to the left! Women to the right!" we read this: "And I did not know that in that place, at that moment, I was parting from my mother and Tzipora forever." No shouting, no breastbeating, only a kind of horrified silence in those words. But a silence which suggests so much.

After being forced to witness a multiple hanging, Wiesel recalls "That night the soup tasted of corpses." He tells of seeing a prisoner killed by his own son over a piece of bread, a son who was then immediately murdered by a group of other prisoners. Wiesel's conclusion: "I was fifteen years old." Who has ever had a teen-aged child who will not be moved by the volumes that those five words contain?

Wiesel's father is murdered. He loses everything—family and spirit, faith and hope. Yet from this devastating position he is resurrected in God as his most recent work, the cantata (on which Darius Milhaud collaborated) *Ani Maamin*, eloquently insists. But on his way to making this supreme poetic act of faith, Wiesel presents us with characters, fictional and historical, who are embodiments of struggle, perseverance, understanding, faith, and love to a degree that no other contemporary novelist in the world is able to achieve.

The painful personal journey through fiction begins with *Dawn*, a novel about a young Jewish boy who must kill a British hostage in retaliation for "crimes" committed by an occupational army in Palestine. It is indeed a father figure that the boy kills and he, in this first person narrative, comes to a realization of the horror of his crime. The boy thinks as he faces the doomed Englishman: "We were alone not only in the cell but in the world as well, he seated, I standing, the victim and the executioner. We were the first—or the last—men of creation; certainly we were alone." As the boy's ancestors parade before him in several mystical scenes he becomes aware that a man hates his enemy because he hates his own hate. And when he kills, he knows he has killed himself. There is no victory in

murder, there is only murder in murder. He also compre-
hends that "we shall be bound together for all eternity by
the tie that binds a victim and his executioner."

Most of all, however, like all of Wiesel's novels, *Dawn* is a
book of questions. "Where is God to be found? In suffering or in rebellion? When is a man most truly a man?
When he submits or when he refuses? Where does suffering lead him? To purification or to bestiality?" For Wiesel, the question is all important. He believes that answers change, only the questions are eternal. He is thus
the archetypal seeker, wandering, seeking to know,
challenging the mysteries of the universe, courageous
enough to follow the questions wherever they may lead
him.

A key work in the Wiesel mosaic is his second novel, *The
Accident*, in which the twin themes of love and knowing
one's self appear. In fact we may conclude with the author
that it is through knowing himself that an individual may
best learn to love. The story centers around a man who is
hit by a car; the circumstances are ambiguous but he
probably was attempting suicide. A woman's love for him
and a man's friendship help him to recover not only physically but emotionally/spiritually as well. When a doctor
learns that Kathleen loves the critically injured man he
tells her: "In that case, there are good reasons not to lose
hope. Love is worth as much as prayer. Sometimes
more." The victim is able to recognize that "I love Kathleen. Therefore life has a meaning, man isn't alone. Love
is the very proof of God's existence." And he is also com-
forted to know that man too is alive. "The proof: he is
capable of friendship." It is the love/friendship axis which
moves all of Elie Wiesel's subsequent fiction while reveal-
ing not only his own soul to us but our own souls as well as
the search for inner discovery which goes ever deeper.

The Town Beyond the Wall could be subtitled "A Tale of
Friendship." In it the main character, Michael, resists

torture as long as possible so that his friend Pedro can escape the authorities. A new fictional theme is introduced, that of madness. Not clinical insanity, of course, but a mystical madness which is clearly sanity in a world gone berserk. We met the historical Moshe the Madman in *Night* and he appears in all of the fictional books—and is the main character in *The Oath*, Wiesel's latest novel.

Michael, in *The Town*, understands that "The man who chooses death is following an impulse of liberation from the self; so is the man who chooses madness." A page later we read: "The choice of madness is an act of courage. It can't be done more than once. It's an end in itself. An act of the free will that destroys freedom. Freedom is given only to man. God is not free." Michael tells a story in this novel in which the hero is "silence." This illustrates rather efficiently what is perhaps Wiesel's most important stylistic achievement, writing in a genre which Ihab Hassan has labeled "the literature of silence."

Partly, at least, this is a literature of understatement. Wiesel is obsessed by the fact that he must tell his tales— as a kind of messenger from the dead—but he fears that his words will be unworthy of the Holocaust victims. They are inadequate, almost lies in comparison to the terrible story that they have to tell. But this modern Ancient Mariner will render his story, as economically as he can, concluding that "God punishes the Jews because he loves them, because he is determined to make them pure and just."

The next tale of friendship (in *The Town* Pedro has discovered that "Friendship is an art") is *The Gates of the Forest*. Here the author's simplicity of narrative technique combines with a renewed emphasis on obliterating temporality which makes past and present nearly one. The presentness of the past, so important to someone like Nikos Kazantzakis, is also important to Wiesel. He knows that each of us is an inheritor of the entire past while being the beginning point for all of the future. Hence the woman or man of integrity is a kind of aleph point, containing all of the universe in a given instant.

The Gates tells of a survivor's trials in not only merely surviving, but in plunging into the depths of his soul in a continual act of self discovery. People sacrifice to save him so that he may learn what he does in the end. He learns (as Camus' character does in *The Plague*) that "He who is not among the victims is with the executioners." But this is a message of hope, not of despair. For as Gregor, the main character can remark to the woman he loves, "The Messiah isn't one man, Clara, he's all men. As long as there are men there will be a Messiah."

There is, perhaps, no more fitting proof to be found of the last sentence than Wiesel gives in *The Jews of Silence*, an account of Soviet Jewry under persecution. In this non-fiction book, a result of a trip to Russia, the author distinguishes two types of silent Jews—those oppressed by persecution and those around the world who are indifferent to the sufferings of other Jews. His sympathy for and portrayal of Russian Jews celebrating a religious holiday, fearlessly and joyfully, is only balanced by the shame and disappointment over that lack of attention free Jews are giving to their brothers and sisters in Russia.

Legends of Our Time is a collection of fifteen memory pieces about the death of Wiesel's father, Moshe the Madman, a visit to Germany where he could not hate, an old teacher, the Eichmann trial, a plea for remembrance of the Holocaust dead. This gathering is as autobiographical as Wiesel is likely to be in print and if one wishes to know the author behind the other volumes, this work must be read. Wiesel here proves that he is as comfortable with the short, non-fiction mode as he is with the regular novel form.

"He who says 'I' has said everything. Just as every man

contains all men, this word contains all men, this word contains all words. It is the only word God uttered at Mount Sinai. Yet one must know how to pronounce it as He does. He says 'I' and it means: I who am with you, within you. We say 'I' and it means: I who am opposed to you, all of you. His 'I' embraces men, ours divides them." With these words, found early in Wiesel's novel *A Beggar in Jerusalem*, a tale of friendship begins. It takes place during what history has labeled the Six-Day War, a time when friendships could become intense, questions about God become increasingly searching, the search for identity more relevant than ever.

We have noted Wiesel on friendship. He adds this: "Loving is a privilege, greater even than being loved. Be proud of it, even if your love is not requited." All of Wiesel's writings, of course, are about man's relation to God. Here may be found his basic appeal to readers. In *Beggar* he tells most succinctly of this relationship: "In the beginning there was the word; the word is the tale of man; and man is the tale of God." And who is the Jew? How is he to be identified, to identify himself? The answer is found in authenticity. " 'We are Jews only by accident; we are men and that is all.' Yet, here they are: Jews again. And men. Because there comes a time when one cannot be a man without assuming the Jewish condition." And later, more specifically, "The Jews are God's memory and the heart of mankind. We do not always know this, but the others do, and that is why they treat us with suspicion and cruelty."

One Generation After is a non-fiction work of explicit memory. It contains recollections of and reflections on the Holocaust. Wiesel is sad, not angry, searching without fully concluding. Again his understatement underlines the mystery of his quest—of the quest of all of us. Wiesel is a man in search of his soul, of mankind's soul. How does one communicate that? This book ends with a sentence that is to be addressed to those who died at Auschwitz, Buchenwald, Dachau, Treblinka, Belsen, Birkenau, Ponar, Majdanek, Sobibor, Mauthausen: "Tell them that silence, more than language, remains the substance and the seal of what was once their universe, and that, like language, it demands to be recognized and transmitted." This mystical silence, this awe before God and the actions of men, is the substance of every line Wiesel has ever written.

Souls on Fire is Wiesel's tribute to Hasidic masters, men as well known to all of us as Israel Baal Shem Tov, and many that few of us will recognize. But each portrait is of a man who disturbed the universe for God. We meet holy men "preferring the poverty of the poor to the poverty of the rich," men of the sacred utterance who comprehended, as surely Wiesel himself does, that "some words *are* deeds." Wiesel's books are deeds.

His most recent novel is *The Oath* and once again it reveals a soul—and once again, if we allow it to, that soul is our very own. Moshe the Madman who is a constant in Wiesel's writings is here, for the first time, a major character. He futilely attempts to sacrifice himself to save a community of Jews from annihilation. In this story of a pogrom Moshe's words reveal Wiesel's vocation. "Jews felt that to forget constituted a crime against memory as well as against justice: whoever forgets became the executioner's accomplice. The executioner kills twice, the second time when he tries to erase the traces of his crimes, the evidence of his cruelty. He must not be allowed to do it, he must not be allowed to do it, we have been saying and repeating throughout the generations. He must not be allowed to kill the dead before our very eyes. We must tell, shake, awaken, alert, repeat over and over again without respite or pause, repeat to the very end these stories that have no end . . ."

Not in spite of all that he has suffered and written, but because of all that he has suffered and written, Elie Wiesel was able to achieve his tremendous act of faith in his cantata *Ani Maamin* with music by Darius Milhaud. I was able to see the world premiere of this work at Carnegie Hall in New York where Jews and non-Jews wept during this search for God and this proclamation of God. The title begins one of the thirteen Articles of Faith set forth by Maimonides which opens thus: "I believe in the coming of the Messiah." It became a hymn for Jews in the camps during World War II and is symbolically perfect for the cantata. Here is the one work in which Wiesel cannot understate. His relation to God he must shout. His hope must be made manifest.

> Auschwitz has killed Jews
> But not their expectation.

In all of his work, Wiesel sees the authentic man as all men, the fully lived moment as eternal. That he has been able to transmit this to us without sentimentality, without exaggeration but always with challenge, with a holy demand, because it is a demand of all men for all men, is remarkable.

Over a half century ago, novelist Henry James insisted that a writer be one on whom nothing is lost. Such an author is Elie Wiesel. He has absorbed the past of a people, their sufferings and their joys, and projected them into a future of Hope. His writings are those of an authentic Jew which means an authentic Man. His reverence for life in a post-Holocaust age (and, again, perhaps a pre-holocaust age) results in a message we must not overlook. It is through *deeds* such as Wiesel's *words* that we may save a world.

This letter of nomination is presumptuously long. Nevertheless I did wish to survey the entire body of Wiesel's work to emphasize what this Jew has meant to be, to a Christian and to me, a literary critic. (I ought to mention, also, his relative popularity among Arab readers—a significant achievement at this time.) Wiesel does no less than splendidly yet simply offer faith to each of us—faith in God and faith in Man. I suggest it would be appropriate, indeed, for his work to be recognized by your Committee.

Thank you.

Peace in deed,

Harry J. Cargas
Coordinator, Humanities Div. IV
(English, Art, Theatre, Music)